# Due Diligence List

# Due Diligence List

www.duediligencelist.com

*Scott S. Pickard*

Writers Club Press
New York  Lincoln  Shanghai

# Due Diligence List
### www.duediligencelist.com

Writers Club Press
an imprint of iUniverse, Inc.

For information address:
iUniverse, Inc.
2021 Pine Lake Road, Suite 100
Lincoln, NE 68512
www.iuniverse.com

ISBN: 0-595-26130-2

Printed in the United States of America

*Due Diligence List* has over 2,000 good due diligence questions organized under fourteen major functional areas of the business. The entire book is also online at **www.duediligencelist.com**. Readers can subscribe free to receive e-notifications when new questions are added to the site.

There is also a sister book, *Leaders Ask Good Questions*, which has the same questions organized alphabetically. *Leaders* is also available in paperback and online at **www.askgoodquestions.com**.

Scott Pickard

# *Contents*

# Corporate Governance

Acquisitions
Annual Report(s)
Annual Shareholder Meeting
Antitrust
Articles of Incorporation
Associations
Board Agenda
Board Audit Committee
Board Committees
Board Compensation Committee
Board Makeup
Board Management
Board Minutes
Board Nominating Committee
Board Performance Evaluation
Board Prerogatives
Board Retreat
Board Tenure
Business Judgment Rule
Charity
Chewable Poison Pill
Common Stock
Conflicts of Interest
Constituencies
Corporate Development Policy
Corporate Governance
Cumulative Voting

Dead-Hand Poison Pill
Director Compensation
Director Support and Training
Directors and Officers Insurance
Diversification
Divestitures
Due Diligence
Enron
Family Business
Goals
Governance
Growth
Insider Trading
Institutional Investors
Investor Relations
Key Indicators
Liquidation and Dissolution
Major Shareholders
Mergers
Milestones
Mission Statement
Outside Directors
Ownership
Poison Pill
Preemptive Rights
RICO
Social Accountability 8000 (SA 8000)
Social Investing
Stockholders
Strategic Alliances
Strategic Planning
S.W.O.T. Analysis
Takeover Defense

Vision Statement
What if?
Women on the Board

## Acquisitions

- Does the company have an analysis of the tax basis of assets being acquired?

- Does the company have an estimate of the fair market value of the assets acquired and liabilities assumed?

- What expense items can be added back to the income statement because the owner has been taking out excessive compensation?

- What is the estimated recapture tax liability, assuming that such is triggered? How does this compare to the present value of step-up benefits?

- Are there deferred intercompany gains or nondeductible write-offs that may result in additional taxes?

- What is the expected transaction effect on net operating loss and tax credit carryovers?

- What are the expected benefits of a taxable vs. nontaxable transaction?

- What is the performance of all operating entities that have been acquired in the past five years?

- Has the company made any bad acquisitions? What is being done to mitigate the adverse impacts?

- Can we maximize the salvage value of certain under-performing assets via a corporate barter transaction?
  [(a)obsolete or excess inventory; (b)services; (c)underutilized plant capacity; (d)excess packaging; (e)short-dated products; (f)returns; (g)refurbished goods.]

# Annual Reports

- What amount is spent each year to produce the annual report? Is it reasonable?
- What shareholder feedback has the company received? Have we acted on it?

# Annual Shareholder Meeting

- Do the by-laws specify cumulative voting?
- Were there any major problems with dissenting stockholders at the last annual shareholders' meeting?
- Are we making it possible for non-attending shareholders to participate in a Web-cast meeting?

# Antitrust

- If the company is dominant in its market, are there any potential antitrust problems?
- Does the company use intellectual property as a club to coerce customers and rivals?
- Is the company slowing innovation in the marketplace by destroying existing or potential competitors?
- Does the company seek interoperability alliances with its competitors? Does this activity violate any antitrust laws?
- Does the company effectively set the technical standards for its industry? Does this then allow the company to exert substantial control over the competition?

# Articles of Incorporation

- Where is the location of the original articles of incorporation?

## Associations

- Does the company sponsor memberships for the board in key associations providing training and resources for directors?

## Board Agenda

- Does the CEO effectively integrate the agenda items of all board members? On both a macro (1-2 year) and micro (meeting-to-meeting) basis?

- How are agenda items prioritized?

- Is the agenda focused on strategic issues that will determine the company's longer-term positioning, or is it delving too deeply into operational details?

## Board Audit Committee

- Is the audit committee failing to perform its job properly because members are either unqualified or are too close (related) to the management of the company?

- Does the committee fully understand and comply with all required SEC reporting requirements?

- Do audit committee members meet the tests for independence necessary to meet SEC guidelines?
  [(a) they, their spouses or children do not currently work or have worked at the company or its affiliates within the past five years; (b) they have not received compensation from the company or its affiliates for work other than board service; (c) they are not partners, shareholders or officers of a business with which the corporation is dealing.]

- Does at least one audit committee member have an accounting or finance background?

# Board Committees

- What are the board's policies for director committee service? [(a) compensation; (b) number of committees at one time; (c) minimum time requirements; (d) tenure on each committee]
- What are the functioning committees of the board?

# Board Compensation Committee

- Is the compensation committee responsible for CEO succession, or has a special committee been formed for this function?

# Board Makeup

- What criteria/objectives are set to establish the makeup of the board?
- Is the size of the board appropriately scaled to the size and scope of the company's operations?
- What are the director profiles needed to compose the board?
- Is the number of inside vs. outside directors balanced?
- What can the board learn from the composition of competitors' boards?
- Does each director have a personal economic stake in the company?
- Is it appropriate and feasible for the board to have directors from other countries?

# Board Management

- What percentage of time does the CEO spend on board-related activities? Is it reasonable?

- Is the board careful to not get involved in micro-managing the operations of the company?

- Instead of hard-copy briefing books, has the board considered developing its own password-protected board Web site as a clearinghouse for all board activities and information?
  [(a) minutes; (b) orientation of outside directors; (c) agendas; (d) financials; (e) committees]

## Board Minutes

- Are all board minutes archived at company headquarters and accessible by directors?

- What target is set for turnaround of board minutes?

## Board Nominating Committee

- Does the board use an executive recruiter to search, screen, and select new director candidates?

- Is the nominating committee applying the rule of "least conflicts and the most information" when evaluating top director candidates?

- Is the company carrying adequate directors and officers (D&O) liability insurance? How has this affected the attraction and retention of high-quality directors to the board?

## Board Performance Evaluation

- How is board performance measured? How often?

- Does the board perform a self-evaluation on an annual basis?

- Does management evaluate the board?

- Based on the most recent evaluation, does the board contain the right individuals to provide effective oversight for the current and future needs of the company?

## Board Prerogatives

- Do the board and management clearly understand and agree to those decisions and rights the board chooses to reserve to itself? [(a) strategic plan approval; (b) deal size limits; (c) sale of company assets; (d) reporting of buyer inquiries; (e) opinion letter; (f) takeover defense; (g) other deal-related issues; (h) acceptable dilution ratios; (i) valuation methods; (j) limits on investment banking fees; (k) requirements for post-deal audits]
- Has the board specified a transaction level or size which requires board review and approval?
- What is the board's policy on the use of stock for mergers and acquisitions?
- How far can management proceed with the exploration of the sale of assets without board approval?
- What is the board's policy on management's obligation to promptly report all inquiries concerning significant transactions?
- Do employees know how to respond to unsolicited inquiries?
- What is the board's policy on when an opinion letter should be required? What transaction size?
- Who will sign off on valuation?
- Who will approve letters of intent?
- Who will approve investment banking fees?
- Who will approve deal structuring?

# Board Retreat

- Does the board conduct a strategic planning retreat separate from the normal planning activities of corporate staff?
- How is the board's strategic planning output integrated with the staff's?

# Board Tenure

- What is the mandatory retirement age for directors?
- What is the term limit for directors?

# Business Judgment Rule

- Does the board have a consensus understanding of a working definition and application of the business judgment rule as it relates to the board's function and obligations?

# Charity

- Is the company verifying the credibility and solvency of all charities receiving a donation?

# Chewable Poison Pill

- Has the board considered a "chewable poison pill" structured so that the pill's barrier to an unsolicited takeover disappears after an all-cash for all shares takeover offer of at least 25% more than the company's current stock price?

# Common Stock

- What is the number of shares authorized?
- What is the number of shares outstanding?

- Do any restrictions exist on any of the company's common stock?

- Do any options or rights of first refusal exist on any of the company's common stock?

## Conflicts of Interest

- Do any affiliated transactions exist between the company and any of its officers, directors, or their relatives other than in their capacity as an officer or director?

- Do any stockholders supply products and/or services to the company?

- Do any directors supply products and/or services to the company?

- Is General Counsel to the company also a director? Does this pose an unmanageable conflict of interest in the event of a lawsuit against the company? Could this negatively infringe on the attorney-client privilege? Would the company/board be better served to have general counsel serve as corporate secretary instead of director, so that counsel's input can still be heard on important issues?

## Constituencies

- Do management and the board appropriately consider and attend to the interests of all of the company's constituencies? [(a) communities; (b) customers; (c) employees; (d) governments; (e) shareholders; (f) suppliers]

## Corporate Development Policy

- Has the board developed a formal corporate development policy?

[(a) mergers and acquisitions; (b) divestitures; (c) licensing; (d) joint ventures; (e) other external growth structures]

- Has the board clarified the responsibilities of officers and other members of management?

- Is there an internal management committee for reviewing all transactions before board review and approval?

- What controls are in place to ensure management's compliance with the corporate development policy?
  [(a) copies of all policies and procedures; (b) early feedback to management in the deal life cycle; (c) list of alternative strategies that were rejected; (d) designate an internal champion; (e) post-deal audits]

- If the transaction is not approved, what will management do?

## Corporate Governance

- Is the board making full use of the leading corporate governance organizations and resources?

## Cumulative Voting

- Do the by-laws of the corporation call for cumulative voting in all elections for directors?
  [In all elections for directors, every shareholder shall have the right to vote in person or by proxy, the number of shares owned by him/her, for as many persons as there are directors to be elected, or to cumulate such votes, and give one candidate as many votes as the number of directors multiplied by the number of his/her shares shall equal, or to distribute them on the same principle among as many candidates as he/she shall think fit.]

# Dead-Hand Poison Pill

- Should the board consider rescinding its dead-hand poison pill? [Directors ousted in a proxy fight are the only ones empowered to rescind the poison pill and sell the company.]

# Director Compensation

- Are director's fees paid at each board meeting? How much?

- Are directors also offered stock options? Under what plan?

# Director Support and Training

- Does the board consider it appropriate for outside directors to seek independent legal advice to prepare for certain board issues/meetings? Will the company reimburse the director for those charges?

- Does the board have a regular schedule of manager presentations designed to orient outside directors as much as possible to the company?

# Directors and Officers Insurance

- Does the company need to carry Indemnification Insurance for directors?

- Does the company need to carry D& O Liability Insurance?

- Does the company need to carry Health, Life, or Disability insurance for directors?

# Diversification

- Does the organization have a strategic plan of diversification and expansion to mitigate risk and increase revenues and profits?

## Divestitures

- What was the gain (loss) on all divestitures in the last five years?

## Due Diligence

- Is the company disciplined and thorough in its due diligence process when evaluating a candidate for merger, acquisition, joint venture, or strategic alliance?
  [(a) history; (b) principals; (c) affiliates; (d) financials; (e) customers; (f) references]

## Enron

- Have we done, or are we doing anything that can result in an Enron-style financial collapse?
  [(a) self-dealing; (b) undisclosed insider trading; (c) unauthorized compensation; (d) debt-loaded limited partnerships]

## Family Business

- Is the board in-effect controlled by one dominant family member? Is this situation dysfunctional towards good governance?

## Goals

- What are the top five strategic goals for this fiscal year?
- What is the one big audacious goal the company has set for the next 3-5 years?

## Governance

- Who owns the corporation?
- Who has the authority to run the corporation?

- Is it appropriate and feasible for the board to adopt the corporate governance model promoted by the California Public Employee's Retirement System (CalPERS)?
  [(a) accountability to shareholders; (b) transparency of operations; (c) equitable treatment of all shareholders; (d) fair and efficient proxy voting; (e) development of market-specific codes of best practice]

# Growth

- Are the necessary internal attributes for growth present in the company?
  [(1) A management team fully committed to growing the business; (2) Intimate awareness of why customers buy its products or services; (3) Very strong cultural values; (4) Superior product or service quality, compared to competitors; (5) Strong strategic relationships with customers and suppliers; (6) Ability to attract and retain talented, dedicated employees better than competitors; (7) Clear understanding of where the customer base and markets are heading; (8) A structured process for developing an effective strategic plan; (9) Well-defined, efficient core business processes; (10) Perception of the strategic plan as a very valuable tool; (11) A clearly defined incentive compensation system; (12) A clearly defined technology and Internet strategy; (13) Excellent channels for distribution of products and services; (14) Regular tracking and monitoring of company and individual performance measures]

- What is the company's annualized rate of growth in net revenues in the last five years?

- What is the company doing to sustain its growth rate?

- Is there a model for this kind of growth in the industry?

- What methodology is used to forecast growth?
  [(a) regression analysis; (b) trend extrapolation; (c) economic

and /or industry indicators; (d) market studies; (e) management estimate]

- Will the projected rate of growth require extraordinary capital infusion or other extraordinary inputs or changes?

## Insider Trading

- Has the company made a reasonable effort to make all insiders (executives, employees, directors) aware of the insider trading rules?

  **Inside information**—News that hasn't been publicly released that would affect a shareholder's decision to buy or sell stock in a publicly traded company.

  **Tipper**—Someone who passes on inside information ("material nonpublic info") that they had a legal obligation to keep secret, but doesn't trade on it themselves.

  **Tippee**—Someone who accepts inside information from a person who shouldn't have revealed it, and trades on it.

## Institutional Investors

- Do institutional investors play a special role on the board of the company? Active or passive?

- What is their impact on management?

## Investor Relations

- Has the company developed an investor relations section within its corporate Web site for investors and the financial community at large?

  [(a)stock quotes; (b) historical stock chart; (c) fundamentals; (d) press releases; (e) quarterly earnings reports; (f) president's letter to shareholders; (g) annual report; (h) SEC filings; (i) analyst reports; (j) First Call consensus earnings estimates; (k) corporate overview; (l) calendar of events; (m) contact information]

## Key Indicators

- Are key indicators being effectively communicated to staff and the board? How?

## Liquidation and Dissolution

- Has the company's attorney developed a detailed checklist and plan for liquidation and dissolution?

## Major Shareholders

- Is the process of selecting new board members substantially driven by a major shareholder(s)? Is this in the best interests of the company?
- Who owns more than 5% of the outstanding common stock?

## Mergers

- Is there an outstanding contractual agreement to merge this company?
- Can the company be sold if it gets into trouble?
- Is there a ready buyer for the company?
- What strategic objectives will this merger accomplish?
  [(a) obtain a leading position in an industry new to the company; (b) become the major player in an industry through merger with a competitor or otherwise; (c) realize high growth, especially in industries not experiencing rapid technological change.]

# Milestones

- Is there an historian for the company?
- Does the company keep an up-to-date chronological listing of all major milestones since incorporation?

# Mission Statement

- Do employees understand the mission of the company?
- Does management feel it is doing a good job of ensuring that individual and department goals support company goals?

# Outside Directors

- As an outside director, have you achieved the proper balance of focus and accountability in your relationship with the CEO?
- Does the board clearly recognize a lead outside director?
- Does the board have an appropriate balance of inside to outside directors?
- Are outside directors holding separate executive sessions as required?
- Are outside directors given unrestricted access to auditors, counsel, and senior management?
- Are the audit, nominating, and compensation committees composed of the appropriate number of outside directors?
- Have outside directors been given primary responsibility for overseeing CEO succession?

# Ownership

- What are the details of all changes in ownership within the last five years?

## Poison Pill

- Has the company put in place antitakeover mechanisms?

## Preemptive Rights

- What preemptive rights exist with all outstanding securities?
- What put/call rights are outstanding?

## RICO

- Does management clearly understand how the federal RICO statute can be applied to a corporate setting?

- Is there anything being done by the company, or an individual employed by the company, which could expose management and/or the board to liability?

## Social Accountability 8000 (SA 8000)

- Is it appropriate and feasible for the company to achieve substantial compliance with the consensus standard SA 8000?
  [(a) child labor; (b) forced labor; (c) health and safety; (d) freedom of association; (e) right to collective barraging; (f) discrimination; (g) disciplinary practices; (h) work hours; (i) compensation; (j) management systems]

## Social Investing

- Has the board developed an investment policy with respect to investing a percentage of its social choice account assets in companies that are models of social and environmental responsibility?

# Stockholders

- Does the company have a complete shareholders list?
- Do the current directors and executive officers own, in aggregate, a majority of the outstanding shares of the corporation?
- Is the company responsive to shareholders?
- Is the process of selecting new board members substantially driven by a major shareholder(s)? Is this in the best interests of the company?

# Strategic Alliances

- What are management's plans for developing strategic alliances to maximize profits and reduce costs?
- What are the risks and how are they controlled?

# Strategic Planning

- What is the process the company follows for annual strategic planning?
- Does management effectively include directors in the strategic planning process?
- Has the board rejected any major proposals by management? Which ones and why?
- Does the company have an effective set of strategic planning guidelines to help managers with this process?
- Does the company use a third-party professional to facilitate the strategic planning process?
- Is the company careful to not over commit to too many strategies? What will be the main focus of the company in the next five years?

- What is the added value of strategic planning?
- Does the company conduct a S.W.O.T. analysis across functional, divisional, and product levels?
[(a) Strengths; (b) Weaknesses; (c) Opportunities; (d) Threats]
- What strategic blunders can the company admit to? What is being done to mitigate the adverse impacts?
- Besides traditional financial measures, what other information does the board study as good indicators of future performance?
[(a) customer satisfaction; (b) competitive cost performance; (c) factors of production; (d) innovation; (e) market position; (f) product or service quality]

## S.W.O.T. Analysis

- What are the three top strengths in the company?
- What are the three top weaknesses in the company?
- What are the three top opportunities in the company?
- What are the three top threats in the company?

## Takeover Defense

- What antitakeover protection plans has the board prepared?
[(a) staggered boards; (b) poison pills; (c) golden parachutes; (d) change of incorporation]

## Vision Statement

- Do employees understand the vision of the company?

## What if?

- What if we lose our CEO tomorrow? What's our plan?

- What if there is a "run on the bank"? Can we survive?
- What if the two major shareholders divorce? Are buy-sell agreements in place?

## Women on the Board

- Is it difficult to recruit women to the board? Why?
- What does the company need to do to make it more attractive to women to serve on the company's board?
- Will the dynamics of the board change with more women? How?

# Engineering / R&D

Billable Capacity
Complexity
Continuous Improvement
Core Competency
Core Technology
Creativity
Design
Engineering
Extreme Rapid Application Development (XRAD)
Innovation
Nanotechnology
Patents
Product Engineering
Professional Services Automation (PSA)
Project Management
Prototyping
Research and Development
Research Ratios
Reverse Engineering
Simulations
Software Development
Software Tools
Standardization
Technology
Technology Transfer
Value Engineering

# Billable Capacity

- How does the company optimize the billable time among all its billable employees?
- How are billable rates determined?
- Will the market bear higher rates?
- Is the company's total cumulative billable competitive with industry norms?

# Complexity

- How many component parts and raw materials are used in the production process?
- How many parts or components are available from only one supplier?
- What are the lead times for critical components?

# Continuous Improvement

- Has the company conducted any time and motion studies? What were the results and recommendations? Any implementations?
- Has the company conducted any production time reduction studies? What were the results and recommendations? Any implementations?
- Has the company conducted any plant layout and utilization studies? What were the results and recommendations? Any implementations?
- Does the company have a regular process of scanning the entire company's inventory of equipment and processes for obsolescence?

- Does the company review long-term contracts on some cycle for all suppliers?
  [(a) suppliers; (b) insurance vendors; (c) banking relationships]

## Core Competency

- What constitutes a core business?
  [(a) product; (b) intellectual property; (c) process; (d) business design]

- What are the corporation's core competencies? Are the company's strategies tightly coupled to these core competencies?

- How visible is the core competency outside the corporation?

- Can competitors easily replicate this core competency? Can the company protect against this?

- Has, or could outsourcing certain functions enable the company to better focus on its core business?

- To focus more on market differentiating processes and technology, is the company evaluating all those high-cost, non-differentiating operational processes that could be shared with other companies in the same industry as a Business Process Utility (BPU)?
  Example: As SABRE was to the airline industry.

## Core Technology

- What is the corporation's core technology?

- How visible is the core technology outside the corporation?

- Can competitors easily replicate this core technology? Can the company protect against this?

- What is the company doing to protect its core technology?
  [(a) aggressive patent application and protection; (b) know-how secrecy; (c) competitive information]

- In what ways is the company leveraging its core technology? [(a) new markets; (b) new materials; (c) new products; (d) new applications; (e) new systems; (f) new partners; (g) new sales channels; (h) new production technology]

## Creativity

- How is creativity fostered in the company?
- Do our competitors have an advantage in this area? Why?

## Design

- Is the company employing web-based collaborative design concepts that ensure its products are manufacturable across the supply chain; are optimized for manufacturing time and costs; and validate supplier capability and availability?

## Engineering

- What is the function of engineering within the overall corporate strategy?
- What is the relationship with production operations?
- How are engineering projects organized and monitored?
- How are engineering efficiency and productivity measured?
- What is the record with respect to engineering projects being completed on time?
- Does the company's engineering department pursue perfectionism to the point where products are not getting to market when they should?

# Extreme Rapid Application Development (XRAD)

- Is IT employing self-constructing XML-based database systems to accelerate the development, prototyping, and deploying of new business applications?

# Innovation

- How is innovation fostered within the company?

- What percentage of revenues is from new products introduced in the last two years?

- Is innovation blocked or stagnated in the company? Why?
  [(a) too many layers of approval required; (b) bad decisions due to lack of info flow up thorough the organization; (c) unsynchronized incentive systems; (d) slow response time to customers and market; (e) "not invented here" syndrome; (f) "always done it this way" syndrome; (g) creativity and innovation are driven underground; (h) overall frustration and dissatisfaction; (i) customers are angry and alienated]

- How fast can a new idea be tried out at the company? Months? Weeks? Days? Hours?

# Nanotechnology

- How can the company exploit, or be affected by, the new nano-technology?

# Patents

- Are the company's products patentable?

- What are the expiration dates on key patents?

- Is the company pursuing, or does it need to pursue, any patent infringement enforcement actions?

- Has the company, or is the company currently, infringing upon any patents? Any threat of a lawsuit?
- Is patenting a cost-effective strategy for the company's products?

## Product Engineering

- Is the Chief Engineer a "registered professional engineer" in the headquarters' state? Other states?
- Are there engineering plans in progress for each product?
- Does the product require customization for each customer? What is customization's percentage of the total cost-of-goods sold?
- Can the product(s) be reengineering and marketed in such a way as to be mass-produced?
- Is the company making maximum use of computer-aided design (CAD) and other software tools to shorten the total new product design and development life cycle?
- What new product plans does the company have?
- Is engineering developing innovative or "me-too" products?

## Professional Services Automation (PSA)

- Is the company replicating its project management systems on a Web-based platform?

## Project Management

- How are costs monitored and controlled?
- Does the company utilize a project management software system?

- What is the record for project completion within budget and schedule?
- Does the company have a project management training program?
- Does the company separate the responsibility for billing from project management?
- Does the company follow a detailed project termination checklist to close out each project?

# Prototyping

- Is engineering taking advantage of state-of-the-art rapid prototyping methods?

# Research and Development

- How are projects chosen for R&D?
- What is R&D's past record for successful completion of projects to budget and schedule?
- When does management expect products will reach the market from research projects currently underway?
- Is the company working smart to optimize the FDA approval process?
- How would management rate the company's R&D operations against its competitors?
- How well does R&D integrate its work with marketing? End user? Engineering? Production?
- Is R&D's major emphasis applied or basic research?
- How much do the company's projected financials depend upon successful new products developed by R&D?

- Does the company effectively protect the secrecy of R&D projects?

- Is there sufficient financing to support R&D at adequate levels?

- What is the company's approach towards capitalization of R&D expenses?

- Is management well informed of R&D activities?

- Are the company's research facilities adequate?

- How confident is management that R&D's team and plan will lead to the right product(s) at the right time?

- Has management evaluated the cost-effectiveness of shifting some portion of R&D expenditures and operations to external sources?
  [(a) venture capital funds; (b) R&D alliances; (c) government funding such as ATP]

## Research Ratios

- How do the company's ratios compare with industry norms?

- What is the three-year trend in these ratios?

- [($R&D expenditures) / ($Total sales)] %

- [($R&D payroll) / ($Total payroll)] %

## Reverse Engineering

- Has the company reverse engineered any competing products?

- Is the company aware of any of its products being reverse engineered by competitors?

# Simulations

- Does the company take advantage of software simulation tools to model and predict outcomes in mission-critical situations for the company?
  [(a) Post-Y2K; (b) Competitive positioning; (c) market pricing; (d) disasters; (e) the Web]

# Software Development

- Does the company have a network-based software configuration management system to control its software development projects?

# Software Tools

- Is the company making maximum use of state-of-the-art software tools to enhance the productivity and quality of every function?

# Standardization

- What programs exist for increasing standardization and ensuring quality control?

# Technology

- Where does the company choose to position itself on the technology application spectrum?
  [(a) exotic, new, very high added-value; (b) specialty, niche products; (c) commodities]

- Is the company effectively focusing its core competencies and technologies to applications that fit its chosen technology spectrum?

- What is the company doing to maintain or improve its technology position?
[(a) R&D investment; (b) production investment; (c) marketing and distribution development]

- Has the company coasted too long in a technology comfort zone?

- Is management evaluating the replacement of declining-margin products with higher-margin products?

- What changes in technology does management foresee in the future? How will this impact the company?

## Technology Transfer

- Does management have a clear strategy for value development of its core technologies?

## Value Engineering

- Does the company practice value engineering? Where, and at what stages?

# Facilities & Equipment

Branch Offices
Energy Requirements
Facilities
Land
Location
Questions for Landlord(s)
Real Estate Holdings
Siting of Facilities
Telecommunications
Videoconferencing
Warehouse Management

## Branch Offices

- How often does the company evaluate the cost-effectiveness of its branch office(s)? How is this done?

## Energy Requirements

- What percentage of operating costs is accounted for by energy purchases?

- Is the processing of any raw materials heavily dependent on energy?

- What kinds of fuel does the company use?

- What is the name and location of energy suppliers?

- Do firm contracts or other commitments exist?

- Is the company or any of its suppliers subject to allocation regulations? Does this affect the company's ability to maintain production levels?

- What is the outlook for energy supplies in areas where the company operates?

- What ability does the company have to pass increased costs on to its customers without losing market share?

# Facilities

- Are the facilities adequate overall to meet the company's objectives?

- Is the company taking advantage of cost-effective, centralized web-based systems that can remotely monitor vital sign data, audio, and video of equipment, facilities, and personnel?

# Land

- Is land an appreciating asset for the company?

- Should the company own or lease the necessary land assets for production and operations?

# Location

- Is it difficult to attract new personnel to this location?

# Questions for Landlord(s)

- How long have you been renting to the company?

- How many square feet does the company rent from you?

- Does the company make its rent payments on time? Have you ever had to contact the company to get your payment?

- Does the company maintain the property in good condition?
- Would you rent to the company again?

## Real Estate Holdings

- Can the board see a complete listing of all real estate holdings, both owned and leased?
- In the event of due diligence on the company, are copies of all executed property leases and property purchase agreements in one reasonably accessible location? Also real estate tax bills?
- Does the company maintain current appraisals on all real estate holdings?

## Siting of Facilities

- In evaluating expansion sites, does the company consider the direct and indirect costs from: earthquakes; hurricanes; tornadoes; extreme cold and heat; lost productivity from snow days and floods?

## Telecommunications

- Does the organization have the ability to **manage, track, audit and plan** the communication's environment across the entire organization at the required level of detail?
  [(a) committed inventory: (b) carrier bills; (c) rates; (d) contracts; (e) Service Level Agreements]

## Videoconferencing

- Has the company explored the benefits of life-sized managed video teleconferencing facilities?

# Warehouse Management

- Is the organization's warehouse management function employing state-of-the-art web-based systems?

# *Finance*

Accountant
Accounting Policies
Accounts Payable
Accounts Receivable
Accrued Liabilities
Accumulated Earnings Tax
Asset Management
Asset Purchase
Audits
Balance Sheet
Bank(s)
Bond Offering
Break-even Analysis
Budgeting
Buy-Sell Agreement
Capital Expenditures
Capitalization
Capitalization of Software
Cash Flow
Cash Management
Contingent Liabilities
Cost-of-Goods Sold
Currency Fluctuations
Customer Credit
Debt
Deflation
Depreciation

Derivatives
Dividend Policy
Equity Financing
Equity Repurchase Agreements
Euro
EVA
Expense Control
Federal Income Tax
Financial Ratios
Financial Statements
Financings
Hedge Fund
Income Taxes
Inflation
Initial Public Offering (IPO)
Intangible Assets
Integrated Spreadsheet™
Intercompany Transactions
Interest Income
Internal Revenue Service (IRS)
Inventory
Investment Analysts
Investment Banker
Investment Policies
Liabilities
Long-Term Debt
Marketable Securities
Micropayments
Net Earnings
Notes Receivable
Operating Profit
Payables
Payroll

Payroll Withholding Taxes
Preferred Stock
Private Placement Memorandum
Profitability
Projected Financial Statements
Quarterly Operating Results
Questions for Accountants
Questions for Banker(s)
Ratio Analysis
Recession
Return on Investment (ROI)
Reverse Merger
Reverse Stock Split
S Corporation
Safe Deposit Box
Sales Taxes
Sarbanes-Oxley Act
SBIR (Small Business Innovation Grant)
SEC (Securities and Exchange Commission)
Sensitivity Analysis
SPE (Special Purpose Entity)
Spreadsheet
State and Local Income Taxes
Stock Offering
Stock Options
Stock Price
Stockholders' Equity
Tax Breaks
Taxes
Treasury Stock
Undervalued Assets
Valuation
Venture Capitalists

Working Capital
Writedowns
Z-Score

# Accountant

- What is the trend for the last three years for total annual outside accounting fees as a percentage of revenues?

- Does the company and/or our accountant have access to comprehensive and up-to-date resources on all accounting and tax-related matters?

# Accounting Policies

- Have there been any significant changes in accounting principles, policies or estimates over the past three years?

- Are there any **accounting policies unique to the company's industry**?

- Are there any proposed changes to generally accepted accounting principles (GAAP) or government regulations that may have a significant impact on the company?

- What are the details of overhead allocation?

# Accounts Payable

- Does any one creditor hold 5% or more of the current total accounts payable?

# Accounts Receivable

- What is the **revenue recognition policy** for recording revenues and establishing receivables?

- Is the distribution of aged receivables under control?

- Is there any one receivable that is 20% or greater of total receivables?
- How often are accounts receivable aging schedules prepared?
- Does the board audit this schedule from time to time?
- How long are accounts permitted to go unpaid before being considered delinquent?
- Are there accounts receivables that represent conditional sales?
- Are any receivables under dispute?
- What percentage of receivables is estimated to be written off at year-end?
- How is bad debt reserve computed?
- How is sales return reserve computed?
- What collection procedures does the company employ?
- Does marketing assist with accounts receivables collections?
- Which receivables are factored? Why? With whom and under what terms?

## Accrued Liabilities

- What are the accrued liabilities outstanding and how did they arise? Are they accounted for properly according to GAAP?
- Has the company accrued all liabilities that it should?
  [a] professional fees; (b) employee benefits; (c) payroll taxes; (d) vacation pay; (e) claims; (f) severance; (g) retirement benefits; (h) warranty costs; (i) pension liabilities; (j) utilities.]

## Accumulated Earnings Tax

- Is the company in danger of triggering an accumulated earnings tax?

- What steps could be taken to prevent or mitigate triggering this tax?

## Asset Management

- How does the organization inventory, track, and manage its hardware and software assets? Is it an effective system that easily scales with the growth of the company?

## Asset Purchase

- Will the seller be able to assume all debt not taken in an asset purchase?
- Are all assets appraised as to current market or liquidation value?

## Audits

- When was the last financial audit performed by an outside third party? For what reason?

## Balance Sheet

- How clean and transparent is the company's balance sheet? Is it where it should be? What corrections and improvements need to be made?

## Banks

- Who is the company's primary bank?
- How many banks does the company have relationships with?
- Who in the company has lead responsibility for banking relationships?
- What is the bank's last credit rating of the company?

- What is the bank's computed Z score?
- Have any banks refused to lend to the company?
- What are the major covenants in loan agreements that give the bank(s) substantial control under certain conditions?
- Is the company in default of any provisions?

# Bond Offering

- What is the company's bond rating? Has it been reviewed or changed recently by Standard & Poor's or Moody's?
- What is the company doing to improve its bond rating?
- Has the company issued high-yield, non-investment-grade bonds? When do these bonds mature?
- Is there adequate cash flow now and in the future to cover interest payments on this debt?
- What were the results of a bond offering in the past year? How was it accepted by the investor community?
- Is the market right for a bond offering?

# Break-Even Analysis

- What are the fixed and variable components of all overhead expenses?
- What is breakeven in sales dollars for each product? Breakeven in units?
- After reaching breakeven, what is the incremental pre-tax profit on a $1 increase in sales for each product?

# Budgeting

- What is the budgeting process at the company?

- How often are budgets assembled?

- How are corporate objectives integrated with the budgeting process?

- Is the budgeting process an interactive one that allows for feedback and coordination between top management and line managers?

- How does the company integrate the individual forecasts of all functional departments into the overall sales forecasting process?

- How has historical performance compared with past budgets?

- How often is performance measured relative to budget?

- How is overall coordination between budgeted goals and operations achieved?

- What kind of accountability procedures does the company employ?

- Does the company have a contingency plan in the event actual results vary significantly from the budget?

- Has management considered transitioning to rolling forecasts rather than annual budgets? Are the enterprise systems in place to accomplish this?

## Buy-Sell Agreement

- Are key components of the buy-sell agreement updated to reflect changing conditions?
  [(a) objectives; (b) valuation process; (c) funding mechanism (cash flow or life insurance proceeds); (d) payment terms (upfront; amortized; interest-only + balloon)]

## Capital Expenditures

- What is the formal procedure for approving major capital expenditures?

- Does the company require any major capital expenditures in the next 12-24 months? What will be the cost?

- How will these expenditures be financed?

- What is the expected return-on-investment (ROI) over the next 3-5 years for each major expenditure?

- If the budget would allow, what equipment should be replaced to either maintain or improve production efficiency, or as protection against major production stoppages should this equipment fail?

# Capitalization

- Does the company maintain an accurate history of the total capitalization of the company (debt and equity) beginning with incorporation?

- Are interest rates such that this would be a good time to consider some debt restructuring?

- Who will put up more cash if the company needs it?

# Capitalization of Software

- To what extent does the company capitalize its software development projects?

- Is the methodology of capitalization well documented and defensible?

# Cash Flow

- How does the company forecast cash flow? How often?

- What are the long-term cash needs for the company for the purchase of property and equipment?

# Cash Management

- Are we reviewing invoices for accuracy so that they match the goods/services and terms which the customer expects to receive?

- Do we anticipate key receipt due dates and call to confirm payment prior to the due date?

- Do we designate a key person to be in charge of cash receipts and disbursements processing? Do they daily identify receipt delays?

- Can customers pay by credit card or by wire transfer (ACH)?

- Do we have our lock box receipts imaged at the lock box location? Is the imaged file transmitted for cash posting?

- What anti-check fraud procedures are in place?

- Do we use Official Bank Checks (OBC)? Do we use plain paper check stock?

- Are all bank accounts reconciled each month? Any discrepancies?

- How does the company forecast cash flow?

- What minimum cash balance is appropriate for the company?

- Is the company using every available technique to minimize transfer time for collecting cash balances?
  [(a) rapid billing; (b) lock boxes; (c)discount policy; (d) collection efforts]

- Who is authorized to make payments of company funds and what amounts are they authorized to disburse?

- Are authorized persons bonded at the appropriate amounts?

- Is the company taking advantage of discounts when available?

# Contingent Liabilities

- Are there any contingent liabilities not shown or footnoted on the balance sheet?
  [(a) warranties; (b) patent infringements; (c) loss contracts; (d) unaccrued compensation for services; (e) contracts subject to termination or renegotiations]

# Cost-of-Goods Sold

- How are product costs established?

- How does the company accurately capture its direct labor costs?

- How does the company monitor and control the costs of production? What has been the trend in the past five years for production costs? For the next five?

- What is customization's percentage of the total cost-of-goods sold?

# Currency Fluctuations

- What has been the impact of the fluctuating value of the dollar on the company's import and export activities?

- What protective measures does the company take against currency fluctuations?

- What exploitive measures does the company take with respect to currency fluctuations?

# Customer Credit

- What percentage of sales is on a credit basis?

- How does the credit approval process work?

- Who establishes the credit limits for customers?

- What percentage of sales were credit losses in previous years?

# Debt

- Do any defaults or violations exist in any of the company's corporate obligations including loan agreements, notes, leases, etc.?

# Deflation

- Does the company foresee a contraction in the general availability of credit or money? If so, would this put noticeable pressure on the pricing of the company's products?

- Has the auction effect of the Web put downward pressure on pricing in the company's market?

# Depreciation

- What depreciation method is used for fixed assets?
- Is the same method used consistently?
- Have any recent changes significantly affected earnings?

# Derivatives

- What is the company's policy on using derivatives to hedge assets, liabilities, and future transactions?

- What is the company's current gain (loss) position on its derivatives?

- Is there any evidence of misuse of derivatives?

# Dividend Policy

- Has the company ever paid cash dividends on its common stock?

# Equity Financing

- What type of equity financing best fits this stage of funding?

- What valuation is being used for this offering?

- What is the investor's IRR based on the company's projected cash returns to the investor?

- Will this return be sufficient relative to the perceived risk of the investor?

- What impact on the distribution of ownership will be effected by the proposed equity financing?

- Is Angel Financing appropriate for this stage of funding?

# Equity Repurchase Agreements

- Are there any puts, calls, or rights of first refusal with any outstanding equity repurchase agreement?

# Euro

- Is the company operating in countries that have adopted the Euro?

- Has the Euro affected the company's European operations? How?

- Will the company need to adopt the Euro as its reporting currency?

- Is the company successfully converting the Euro in its information systems?

- Is the board audit committee prepared for the Euro?

# EVA

- Is it appropriate for management to consider the application of EVA principles in the financial management of the company?

# Expense Control

- Does the company have an ongoing program focused on expense control?
- Has the company implemented a web-based system for enterprise-wide expense control?

# Federal Income Tax

- Have there been any recent examinations by the federal tax authorities? Were there deficiencies? Adjustments?
- Which tax years are open and closed to future tax authority examination?
- Are there any special industry tax considerations of material significance?
  [(a) depletion allowances; (b) special credits; (c) special deductions]
- Does the current income tax reserve cover the current income tax requirements?

# Financial Ratios

- How do the company's ratios compare with industry norms?
- What is the three-year trend in these ratios?
- Gross Margin = [$ Gross Profit / $ Sales] %
- Profit Margin = [$ Net Income Before Tax / $ Sales] %

- Return on Equity = [$ Earnings / $ Total Shareholder Equity] %

- Return on Assets = [$ Earnings / $ Average Total Assets] %

- Current Ratio = [$ Current Assets / $ Current Liabilities]

- Quick Ratio = [$ (Current Assets - Inventory) / $ Current Liabilities]

- Working Capital = [$ Current Assets - $ Current Liabilities]

- Liquidity = [$ Total Assets / $ Total Liabilities]

- Debt/Equity = [$ Total Liabilities / $Total Stockholders' Equity]

- Debt Coverage = [$ EBIT / $ Total Annual Debt Service]

- Cash Flow Cycle = [$ (Receivables + Inventory) / $ Cost-of-Goods Sold]

- Past Due Index = [$ Receivables Past Due / $ Total Receivables]

- Inventory Turns = [$ Cost-of-Goods-Sold / $ Average Inventory Balance]

## Financial Statements

- How soon does the company provide financial statements for the previous month just ended?

- Are there individual financial statements for each major business segment, product line, or geographical location?

- Can a binder be prepared for directors including the annual financial statements for the last five fiscal years? Income statements by month for the most recent two years?

- Is key financial information presented in charts and graphs to improve the interpretation of the numbers?

# Financings

- Does the company need approval of any entity other than the Board of Directors regarding any financing?

- Will the company need to raise any additional capital in the coming year?

- Have significant swings in the company's stock price affected its ability to obtain equity financing?

- Are overseas capital markets a viable source of financing for the company?

- Is the company making use of equipment leasing where it is cost-effective?

# Hedge Fund

- How did the company select this hedge fund?

- How does the company's hedge investment strategy work?

- What are the risks?

- What market conditions favor the fund manager's strategy, and which ones work against it?

- What is the fund manager's experience and track record?

- How long before the company can withdraw its money?

- How is the fund manager being compensated?

# Income Taxes

- Is the company's tax planning adequate?

- Has the company taken advantage of all potential tax savings?

- Are the company's tax basis records in good shape?

# Inflation

- What impact has inflation had in terms of restating inventory costs to current prices?

- What impact has inflation had in terms of restating book value of property, plant, equipment, and leases to replacement value?

- Generally in the last few years, have price increases in the company's products been enough to offset increases in production costs?

- Has the gross profit percentage been maintained?

- In international markets with high-inflationary economies, how does the company protect its assets and earnings?

# Initial Public Offering (IPO)

- Is an IPO a realistic consideration for the company?

- Are the market conditions right for an IPO?

# Intangible Assets

- Has the company documented a description and explanation of how all its intangible assets arose?
  [(a) goodwill; (b) deferred charges; (c) research and development; (d) company costs; (e) patents and trademarks; (f) databases]

# Integrated Spreadsheet™

- Does the company have a spreadsheet tool it updates monthly to project financials and cash flow?

# Intercompany Transactions

- Are there deferred inter-company gains or nondeductible write-offs that may result in additional taxes?

# Interest Income

- What is the company's plan for optimizing the balance between maintaining the liquidity of excess cash vs. generating maximum short-term and long-term interest income?

# Internal Revenue Service (IRS)

- Has the IRS proposed any tax audit adjustments that would adversely affect the company's financial performance?

# Inventory

- What is the location of inventory?
  [(a) on hand; (b) in transit; (c) outside warehouses]
- What inventory valuation method does the company use? How reliable is this procedure?
- When was the book value of inventory last reconciled with the present market value of inventory?
- How much of inventory is pledged as collateral for borrowing?
- Have inventory accounting practices changed recently? What was the effect on earnings and net worth?
- What is the percentage distribution of inventory between raw materials, work in progress, and finished goods? Any trends that have meaning?
- What is the inventory control system?
- What is the inventory reorder procedure?

- How many months of production can be supported by the current inventory level?

- How are usage rates monitored and matched with lead times?

- How is the optimal time and amount of reorders determined?

- How often are physical inventories taken?

- Is the current level of inventory at an optimum level? If not, what changes are needed to maximize efficiencies and minimize storage and transportation costs?

- Are there any inventory items that require delivery lead times of more than thirty days?

- What percentage of the inventory is obsolete, out of style, subject to markdown or complete disposal?

- What is the current inventory turn? Last year?

## Investment Analysts

- Does the company provide earnings forecasts to analysts? To the public?

- How well does the company meet its earnings forecasts?

- What is the current status of the consensus evaluation of the company among investment analysts?

## Investment Banker

- Is any broker entitled to a commission upon successfully raising of capital?

## Investment Policies

- What capital budgeting procedures does the company employ?

- What is the minimum acceptable investment return on capital items?

- Who makes the order decision for production equipment and machinery?

- How are lease vs. purchase decisions evaluated?

- What is the company's investment policy with respect to excess cash?

- How much is kept in short-term marketable securities?

- What is the record of gains (losses) from sales of securities in the company's portfolio? What is the IRR of the portfolio for the last year? The last 3-5 years? Since inception?

## Liabilities

- Do any defaults or violations exist in any of the company's corporate obligations including loan agreements, notes, leases, etc.?

## Long-Term Debt

- Does the company's aggregate of long term debt need to be reviewed and consolidated for more competitive terms/rates?

- Is the company's debt/equity ratio acceptable to its lenders? Other constituencies?

## Marketable Securities

- Does the company perform background checks on either the firms or individuals that handle the company's trading in securities?

# Micropayments

- Does the company's e-commerce division have a mechanism for aggregating small transactions to make it worthwhile to handle?

# Net Earnings

- What is management's forecast for net earnings in this fiscal year?

- What is management's explanation of the forecast's variance to budget?

# Notes Receivable

- Is there a list of notes receivable indicating the terms?

- What is the company's bad debt reserve policy? Is it adequate?

# Operating Profit

- How can the company increase its operating profit?
  [(a) price increases; (b) volume increases; (c) new products or services; (d) operating cost decreases]

# Payables

- Is the company current with all payables?

# Payroll

- Does the company have a written procedure for determining beginning salaries, raises, promotions, etc.?

- Does the company give annual cost-of-living adjustments (COLA)? What was it the last three years?

- Is the company migrating payroll systems to a Web-based platform?

## Payroll Withholding Taxes

- Is the company current with all payroll tax deposits?

- What checks and balances are in place to ensure proper withholding and deposit of all monies withheld from payroll checks? [(a) social security; (b) Medicare; (c) 401-K; (d) cafeteria plan; (e) United Way; (f) other]

## Preferred Stock

- What is the number of shares authorized?

- What is the number of shares outstanding?

- Do preferred stock shareholders have a preference in liquidation, dissolution, or winding up of the affairs of the company?

- Do preferred stock shareholders have preemptive or subscription rights?

- Is each share of preferred convertible into one share of common stock?

## Private Placement Memorandum

- Is the company confident that all relevant disclosures have been made in any private placement memorandum?

- Do subscription agreement(s) clearly disclose all requirements for qualified investors?

- Do investors all meet the tests for accredited investor? [(a) annual income $200,000 or greater; or (b) net worth of $1,000,000; or (c) investment represents 20% or less than net worth]

# Profitability

- Is profitability of individual business units and product lines monitored?

- What is the gross margin on sales?

- Is any one product or division considered the "cash cow"? If not, what are the chances that could happen with an existing product or division, or that opportunities exist to acquire or develop one?

# Projected Financial Statements

- How are financial projections (and assumptions behind them) put together?

- Are they realistic? Is there enough reliable information behind the assumptions to make them believable?

- Who has reviewed the projections?

- Are basic ratios consistent throughout the projections?

- Are basic ratios consistent with industry figures? If not, why?

- How do these projections/assumptions differ with past projections? Did the company achieve past projections? If not, why?

- What are the best-case and worst-case projections?

- What is the probability that the company can meet its projections?

# Quarterly Operating Results

- How volatile is the fluctuation in revenues from quarter to quarter? What are the major reasons for fluctuations in revenues? Is the pattern of quarterly revenues hard to predict? How does the company try to encourage more uniform buying patterns?

- How volatile is the fluctuation in expenses from quarter to quarter?

- How volatile is the fluctuation in profit from quarter to quarter?

## Questions for Accountants

- How long have you been the accountant?

- How long has the lead individual been handling the annual audit?

- Can you verify the numbers in the audit on assets, sales, and profits?

- Are there any significant or material changes in the numbers set up by management and the financial audit?
  [(a) inventory value; (b) quality of receivables; (c) work in progress; (d) cost of goods sold]

- Did you issue a management letter?

- Are the company's books and records in good condition for an efficient audit, or do they need improvement?

- Are adequate controls in place to prevent misuse of funds?

- How would you evaluate the financial management team?

- How would you evaluate the CFO?

- Is the company having operating problems?

- Is management listening to your best advice?

## Questions for Banker(s)

- How long has the company banked with you?

- How long has the current loan officer serviced this account?

- How does the bank rank the credit worthiness of the company?

- What is the current credit limit for the company? What is the lowest and highest credit balance with this bank?
- Has the company ever been denied credit? When and why?
- How is short-term debt collateralized?
- How is long-term debt collateralized?
- Has the company ever been in default on a loan payment(s)?
- Does the company have any operating problems?
- What is your evaluation of management?
- Is management listening to your best advice?

## Ratio Analysis

- How do our key operating ratios compare to last year?
- How do our key operating ratios compare to the industry?

## Recession

- Does management have a financial contingency plan in the event of a recession that adversely impacts the performance of the company?

## Return on Investment (ROI)

- How does the company's return on investment (ROI) compare with other companies in the same industry? Stock value?

## Reverse Merger

- Does a reverse merger make sense for the company? How many of the following criteria does the company match up with?
  [(a) Unique business model, product, or service; (b) Revenues of $3 million + (c) A record of dynamic growth; (d) Positive cash

flow; (e) Plans for $50 million + in revenue; (f) Proven, experienced management team; (g) Buzz in the industry; (h) Strong CFO; (i) Audited, clean financial statements; (j) Sufficient working capital for public company overhead; (k) Access to a reputable, thorough matchmaker/deal maker]

## Reverse Stock Split

- To improve market perceptions, does the company need to consider a reverse stock split to restructure the per-share price upward?

## S Corporation

- Has management studied all the tax ramifications of converting from a C corp to an S corp?

## Safe Deposit Box

- Does the company keep the originals (or copies) of important documents in an off-site safe deposit box?
  [(a) insurance policies; (b) contracts; (c) lease agreements; (d) mortgages; (e) articles of incorporation; (f) software backup tapes]

## Sales Taxes

- Is the company complying with all sales tax regulations?

- What is the status of any sales or excise tax audits?

## Sarbanes-Oxley Act

- Is the company subject to the executive certification requirements?

[ public companies filing quarterly and annual reports with the SEC ]

- Which reports are subject to the requirements?
  [ 10-K | 10-KSB | 10-Q | 10-QSB | 20-F | 40-F ]

- Who are the certifying officers?

- Even though the company is not a publicly listed stock but has issued public debt, is the company still required to comply with the executive certification requirements?

- Are the CEO and CFO current with quarterly and annual filings?

- Do the certifications follow the SEC's prescribed wording verbatim?

- Are the certifying officers being careful to disclose and certify that material non-financial information, as well as financial information, is included in all quarterly and annual reports?

- Do the company's internal controls meet the requirements of the ACT to insure reliability of financial reporting? Are they being evaluated quarterly as required?

- Are effective disclosure controls and procedures in place?
  [(a) oversight committee; (b) standard reporting package; (c) maintained inventory of reporting requirements; (d) defined roles/responsibilities; (e) monitor change; (f) mindset of fair reporting; (g) documentation and communication]

- Are the certifying officers directly involved in the design of disclosure controls and procedures?

- Have the certifying officers developed a rigorous checklist they complete before signing certification?

- What steps are being taken to improve disclosure controls and procedures over the longer term?

- Do the CEO and CFO clearly understand the certification requirements and what they must evaluate?

[(a) disclosure controls; (b) effectiveness; (c) report to auditors and committee; (d) significant changes]

- Do the certifying officers believe the company's current system of internal controls and disclosure is adequate? What is the risk that the SEC may find this as non-responsive?

- Do the certifying officers feel strongly that a "chain of certifications" should be pushed down the hierarchy through key direct reports to management?

- Are the certifying officers using multiple sources of information when assessing disclosure controls?
  [(a) self-assessments; (b) internal auditors; (c) external auditors]

- Are the certifying officers modeling their control framework on COSO's "Internal Control - Integrated Framework"?

- Are the certifying officers reporting all deficiencies found in their evaluation?

- Is management checking for changes to the control system which could be driven by growth, employee and management turnover, downsizing, new systems and infrastructure, M&A activity, and catastrophic events?

- Is the company in compliance with the NYSE's listing requirement for an internal audit function?

- Has the company adopted a code of ethics for senior financial officers?

# SBIR (Small Business Innovation Grant)

- Is the company fully exploiting the use of SBIR grants as a funding source for early-stage R&D?

# SEC (Securities and Exchange Commission)

- Has the CEO filed a disclosure with the SEC certifying last quarter's financials? If not, is there a problem?

# Sensitivity Analysis

- What effect does the variation in key assumptions have on the financial projections?

# SPE (Special Purpose Entity)

- Is the company making use of SPEs? If so, how are they performing?

- What is the company's liability for non-performing SPEs? To what degree is this risk reflected on the company's balance sheet?

- Are there any potential conflicts of interest with respect to company officers and directors also owning shares in these SPEs?

# Spreadsheet

- Does the company provide to the board key spreadsheets and graphs about performance for review and analysis?

# State and Local Income Taxes

- Is the company current on all state and local income taxes?

- Have there been any state tax audits? Any deficiencies? Adjustments?

# Stock Offering

- Is the market right for a stock offering?

- What were the results of a stock offering in the past year? How was it accepted by the investor community?

## Stock Options

- Is a copy of the written stock option plan available for review?

- Are stock options valued by a reputable, third-party professional valuation specialist?

- Has the stock option program been a motivator or de-motivator to key employees?

- Do the provisions for vesting and exercise period need to be reviewed and/or modified?

- Are stock options for executive management contingent on performance standards pegged to stock price?

## Stock Price

- How has the economy affected the market price of the company's stock and its price-to-earnings ratio?

- Does management believe that the company's current market valuation is appropriate?

- What does management believe the appropriate price-to-earnings ratio to be?

- How has the company stock performed as compared with the overall market?

- What steps is the company taking to improve its stock value?

- Have significant swings in the company's stock price affected its ability to obtain equity financing?

# Stockholders' Equity

- Does the company have a list of all classes of stock?
  [(a) type; (b) shares authorized; (c) shares outstanding; (d) voting rights; (e) liquidation preferences; (f) dividends; (g) terms of warrants and options outstanding; (h) major owners, date acquired; (i) market price range; (j) special terms]

- What has been the annualized growth rate in stockholders' equity for the last year? Five years? Ten years? Since incorporation?

- Have any restrictions been violated on any of the issued and outstanding equity securities?

- What is the most significant action taken during the past year to improve stockholder value?

# Tax Breaks

- Have any states offered the company tax breaks and incentive offers to locate in their state? Any municipalities?

# Taxes

- Is the company current on all taxes owed?
  [(a) FICA; (b) federal income; (c) state(s) income; (d) real estate; (e) other]

- Did any new tax regulations have a material impact on last fiscal year's operating results?

- Can management summarize for directors the latest three years of federal and state tax returns, including amended or Net Operating Loss (NOL) carry back returns?

- What is the list of states and foreign countries in which the company does business and where sales/use tax returns are filed?

- What is the status of any tax appeals and litigation?
- Have the auditors confirmed that the reported year-end earnings reconcile to the taxable earnings reported to the IRS?

## Treasury Stock

- What activity has occurred in treasury stock for the past three years?

## Undervalued Assets

- Does the company have any patents, trademarks, copyrights, or licenses that are undervalued?
- Does the company have undervalued real estate or equipment?
- Are inventories understated?
- Are the profit sharing and/or pension plan over funded?

## Valuation

- How does the company value its equity securities?
  [(a) frequency; (b) methodologies; (c) 3rd-party professional; (d) other]
- Is the last valuation report available for review?
- What is the current valuation of the company?

## Venture Capitalists

- Is the company aware of any venture capitalists who have invested in this industry or with competitors?
- Can the company successfully compete for equity financing from venture capital sources?

# Working Capital

- What is the effect of a $1 increase in sales on working capital needs?
- What is the relationship between capital required for fixed assets and sales expansion?

# Writedowns

- Were there any recent write downs that surprised the company? What was the impact to net income?
- Is the company anticipating any significant write downs? What will be the impact to net income?

# Z-Score

- Does the company compute its Z-score the way the bank does?
- Does the company's Z-score rank favorably with the bank?

# Human Resources

Absenteeism
Age Discrimination
American Disabilities Act (ADA)
Communications
Comp Time
Conflict Management
Contract Workers
Corporate Communications
Culture
Dental Benefits
EEOC
E-Learning
Emotional Intelligence (EQ)
Employee Assistance Program
Employee Benefits
Employee Litigation
Employee Morale
Employee Ratios
Employee Retention
Employee Survey
Employees
Employment Agreements
Equal Opportunity
Ethics
401(K) Plan
Health Insurance
Holidays

Incentive Compensation Program
Independent Contractors
Information Sharing
Integration Management
Internal Customers
Knowledge Management
Labor
Layoffs
Lifetime Learning
Loans to Employees
Mobile Workforce
Native Intelligence
Non-Union Shop
Organizational Structure
Organization Chart
Peer Group Feedback
Pension Plan
Performance Appraisals
Productivity
Professional Development
Profit Sharing Plan
Psychological Testing
Race Discrimination Lawsuits
Recognition
Recruiting
Reference Checks
Repetitive Strain Syndrome (RSI)
Restructuring
Resumes
Salary History
Seminars
Severance Payments
Sexual Harassment

Short-Term Disability Insurance
Sick Leave
Training
Union Shop
Vacation Policy
Values
Visas

# Absenteeism

- Does the company treat work environment ergonomics seriously as the most effective proactive program to mitigate workplace absenteeism?

- Based on the current degree of "ergonomics-friendly" at our facilities, how does management assess our liability exposure?

- What **programs and policies** are in place and what programs are planned to mitigate this exposure and reach full compliance with OSHA standards?

# Age Discrimination

- Has the company had any age discrimination lawsuits in the past? Any pending or threatening?

# American Disabilities Act (ADA)

- Is the company in compliance with all applicable provisions of the ADA?

# Communications

- In what ways does management communicate with employees? [(a) e-mail; (b) intranet; (c) memo; (d) newsletter; (e) town hall meeting; (f) walking the hallways]

- How would employees evaluate the effectiveness of these programs?

## Comp Time

- What is the company's policy on "comp time" for salaried employees?

## Conflict Management

- Do the CEO and directors effectively address, utilize, and resolve conflict in the boardroom?

- Is the board rendered dysfunctional due to directors who don't communicate effectively with each other, have difficulty reaching consensus on important issues, and find it impossible to work as a team?

## Contract Workers

- Is the company employing a **web-based system to optimize the procurement** and management of contract labor and consulting services? Does the system seamlessly integrate with key existing enterprise systems?

## Corporate Communications

- Is the company using the full online power of 3-D video, broadband, and streaming media to maximize the effectiveness of internal and external communications?

- Does the company have a means of assessing (in real time) the external impact of its communications efforts?

# Culture

- What adjectives describe the company's culture?
  [(a) brave; (b) competitive; (c) confident; (d) enthusiastic; (e) fair; (f) fast; (g) fun; (h) having presence; (I) restless; (j) smart; (k) well-prepared]

- What are the core values of the company's culture?

- Are employees tolerant of growth and associated chaos?

- What is being done to orient the company's culture to the constant change that technology brings?

- Does the company have fun?

# Dental Benefits

- Has the company evaluated the cost-effectiveness of a direct reimbursement plan?

# EEOC

- Are there any EEOC violations?

- What actions has the company taken to resolve them?

# E-Learning

- Is the company making use of Web-based learning platforms for employees and partners?

# Emotional Intelligence (EQ)

- Is the company measuring the EQ of executives and key employees? How?

- How is EQ being measured, monitored, and used as tool for management and leadership development?

# Employee Assistance Program

- Has the company developed and put in place a confidential employee assistance program?

- What range of personal matters does the program address?
[(a) emotional health; (b) mental health; (c) depression; (d) anxiety; (e) stress; (f) career and workplace counseling; (g) self-improvement; (h) parenting and family; (i) marital/relationship; (j) alcohol abuse; (k) drug abuse; (l) gambling; (m) dependent care; (n) legal assistance; (o) financial assistance]

# Employee Benefits

- In the event of due diligence on the company, are details of existing benefits and their costs reasonably accessible in one location?
[(a) vacation policy; (b) sick pay policy; (c) health insurance; (d) disability insurance; (e) life insurance; (f) bonus policy; (g) pension plan; (h) profit sharing plan; (i) overtime policy; (j) employee loans; (k) non-cash perquisites; (l) relocation policy; (m) severance policy]

- Are these policies detailed in an employee handbook?

- Has the company developed a policy relative to the Family and Medical Leave Act (FMLA)?

# Employee Litigation

- Has employee litigation action occurred in the past two years? Any actions threatened or pending?

- What proactive steps are being taken to mitigate this kind of liability exposure?

# Employee Morale

- Is the attitude and morale of employees good?

- Is there generally a strong work ethic among employees?

- Is there a strong team feeling?

- Is the company's energy and productivity being drained by "turf wars" between departments trying to protect power and resources?

- How strong is the environment of trust in the company?

- What is the level of stress in the company?

- How does the CEO monitor morale?

- What specific methods and techniques has the company found and applied to motivate hourly employees?

# Employee Ratios

- How do the company's ratios compare with industry norms?

- What is the three-year trend in these ratios?

- Average Salary = [($Total Payroll) / (Total # of FTE employees)]

- Payroll Cost = [($Total Payroll & Benefits) / ($Total Sales)] %

- Benefits Cost = [($Total Benefits) / ($Total Payroll)] %

- Employee Turnover = [(# of employees left in 1 year) / (Average # of employees)] %

- Management "Weight" = [(# of managers) / (# of employees including managers)] %

- Productivity = [($Total Sales) / (Average # of employees)]

## Employee Retention

- Does the company have an employee turnover problem in general?

- What has been the turnover in the last two years?

- What percentage of turnover is structural, and what percentage is due to forces in the company which are driving people away? What are the forces that are driving people away?

## Employee Survey

- Does the company annually survey employees to assess their overall morale and job satisfaction?

## Employees

- Does the company maintain a list of all employees with key information?
  [(a) name; (b) social security number; (c) duties; (d) date of hire; (e) current salary; (f) location]

- Are the critical functions staffed with well-qualified people?

- Are there special personnel or skill needs related to technology, marketing, or manufacturing? What are the plans to respond to skill needs or technical obsolescence?

- Is there, or will there be, an excess of manpower in some functional areas?

- Can excess people be retrained and reassigned to other areas?

## Employment Agreements

- Are there any employment agreements which are a problem or could become a problem for the company?

# Equal Opportunity

- What percentage of the company's key positions is held by women? What is the trend?

# Ethics

- What is the day-to-day visibility, awareness, and discussion level of ethics within and outside the company? What are insiders and outsiders saying?

- Has the board adopted an Ethics Policy?

# 401(K) Plan

- Is the company current on its deposit of 401(K) funds?

- Do all employee participants in the plan receive monthly statements on time?

- Has the company ever surveyed employees to determine likes/dislikes in the plan?

- If the number of plan participants is 120 or greater, has an audit been scheduled?

- Can plan participants avail themselves of at least an annual evaluation of their portfolio for risk exposure and over-concentrations in their allocations?

# Health Insurance

- Is extended health care coverage provided or subsidized by the company?

- Is cost/employee in line with industry averages?

# Holidays

- Are employees generally satisfied with the company's policy on holidays?

# Incentive Compensation Program

- Is the company plan periodically reevaluated every 2-5 years?
- Is the plan based on discretionary or specific criteria?
- Are other performance measures besides profit evaluated?
- What is the frequency of bonus distributions?
- What is the minimum amount of bonus distribution?
- Are only salaried employees eligible for the plan? How is eligibility determined?

# Independent Contractors

- Is the company confident that all IRS tests are met for suppliers classified as "independent contractors"?

# Information Sharing

- Is information widely and freely shared throughout the company, fostering a common sense of purpose and organizational goals among employees?

# Integration Management

- Has the company developed an integration management plan for before, during, and after the acquisition?
- Has a lead integration manager been assigned to this project?

# Internal Customers

- Can IT and other internal service functions improve efficiency with a software management system?

# Knowledge Management

- Does the organization have the necessary Web-based systems to capture intellectual capital, develop, and manage a repository of knowledge which allows customer service agents to effectively answer inquiries over the Web and in the contact center?

# Labor

- Is the supply of skilled labor adequate for this industry?

- Are the labor pay rates in this industry competitive with those of other industries?

- What is the company's strategy for the next planned labor union contract negotiations?

- Is the company in compliance with all child labor laws at all of its manufacturing facilities?

# Layoffs

- Does the company anticipate the need for any future layoffs? Will there be any problems?

# Lifetime Learning

- Does the company support lifetime learning programs for employees? How? Is online a cost-effective and feasible alternative means?

## Loans to Employees

- Are there any loans to or from management or key stockholders or employees?

- Can the loans be terminated at any time at the discretion of the board?

## Mobile Workforce

- Is the company taking advantage of wireless and web-based applications that streamline field service operations making routine business processes more efficient, the mobile workforce more productive, and customer service more responsive?

## Native Intelligence

- What incentives do workers have to share their "native intelligence" or "tribal knowledge" of processes, methods, and techniques? Has management and the culture of the company created disincentives?

- What manual and automated recording systems are in place to capture this closely-held knowledge?

## Non-Union Shop

- Have there been any recent attempts to unionize employees?

- What specific plans has the company implemented to reduce the possibility of the employees becoming unionized?

- What significant issues should be addressed with non-union employees?

# Organizational Structure

- Is the organizational structure working within the company?
- What is the level of employee buy-in to the company's efforts to match its structure to the demands of the situation?
- Has the organizational structure been changed too often in the past?
- Are there too many layers of management in the company?

# Organization Chart

- Does the company maintain a current organization chart showing all reporting relationships?
- What is the company's philosophy on making its organization chart accessible to employees? The public?

# Peer Group Feedback

- Are the CEO, COO, CFO, and board taking advantage of the benefits of peer group feedback?

# Pension Plan

- Does the company have any unfunded pension costs?
- Is the pension plan over funded?
- Can money be taken out if need be?
- Does the company have a training program offering employees information on how to invest their 401(K) funds or defined-contribution savings plans?
  [(a) setting goals; (b) evaluating risk tolerance; (c) making pre-retirement plans; (d) allocating investments; (e) rebalancing portfolios]

# Performance Appraisals

- How is performance measured and communicated to employees? What form(s) are used?

# Productivity

- What are the current trends in manufacturing productivity for this industry?
- Do these trends reveal any technical obsolescence in the company's operations?
- Does product design restrict process selection for manufacturing? Is the design conducive to an efficient manufacturing process? Is there good integration between product engineering and manufacturing engineering?
- How well do productivity factors benchmark with competitors?
- What are management's goals to improve productivity? How long will it take to achieve these goals?

# Professional Development

- Has the company evaluated the cost-effectiveness of outsourcing its professional development systems development and support to an online provider?

# Profit Sharing Plan

- What percentage of profits is distributed to employees in the profit sharing plan?

## Psychological Testing

- Is the company using a **web-based system** to manage the psychological testing of employee applicants?

## Race Discrimination Lawsuits

- Has the company had any race discrimination lawsuits in the past? Any pending or threatening?

## Recognition

- What recognition programs are in place? Are they effective?

## Recruiting

- Is the organization taking advantage of web-based systems to background check prospective employees?
- What are the terms of engagement for outside search firms?
- How difficult is it to recruit qualified personnel?
  [(a) competition; (b) salary pressure; (c) location]
- What are the major universities where the company recruits entry-level management and technical talent?
- Does the company use lie detector tests?
- Does the company use psychological profile tests?
- Is the company taking full advantage of Web-based systems to manage the recruiting process?

## Reference Checks

- How thorough is the reference checking when recruiting key staff?

# Repetitive Strain Syndrome (RSI)

- Is RSI becoming a problem for the company?
- Does the company have a safety program in place to mitigate the loss in productivity due to RSI?

# Restructuring

- Has the company fully implemented the restructuring actions previously reported?
- What effect has restructuring had on the company's productivity, operating results, and competitive position in the marketplace?

# Resumes

- Are the resumes of key staff available for review in one presentation document?

# Salary History

- Is there a summary of the salary history for all employees? [(a) date of hire; (b) age; (c) position; (d) base salary; (e) date/% increases]

# Seminars

- Does the company sponsor any training seminars for directors?

# Severance Payments

- Are copies available of any prior severance agreements which contain provisions for employee benefits?
- Are total severance payments under control and reasonable?

## Sexual Harassment

- Does the company have in place a sexual harassment policy that can provide an affirmative defense in the event of suit?

- Does the policy effectively address "quid pro quo" harassment ("this for that")?
  [(a) protected group; (b) unwelcome sexual harassment; (c) based on sex; (d) affected a tangible aspect of employment; (e) employer knew or should have known but took no action]

- Does the policy effectively address "environmental sexual harassment"?
  [(a) verbal; (b) physical; (c) visual]

- Have employees been trained in this policy? Is the process repeated annually?

- Has the company had any sex discrimination lawsuits in the past? Any pending or threatening?

## Short-Term Disability Insurance

- Does the company provide short-term disability insurance?

## Sick Leave

- Is sick leave being abused at the company?

## Training

- Does the company have a formal, written training program for its employees?

- Does the company consciously cross-train employees to mitigate problems from absenteeism or sudden departures of employees?

- Is the company developing Web-based training programs?

# Union Shop

- What percentage of employees is unionized? What is the union(s)?
- When does the present contract(s) expire?
- What issues will be addressed during the renegotiations of expiring contracts?
- Have there been any strikes in the past? Any work stoppage?
- How are grievances handled? How many grievances are outstanding?
- Does the company have a good working relationship with the union leader(s)?
- Is the union due compensation for a planned plant shutdown?
- In management's opinion, have the unions resisted changes to improve productivity in the company?

# Vacation Policy

- Is the company's vacation policy competitive with industry standards?

# Values

- How visible and well understood are the values of the corporation among management and employees?

# Visas

- Does the company provide reasonable assistance and expense reimbursement to obtain work visas for key technical and management employees?

- What percentage of employees is working under a visa of some form?

- How difficult would it be to replace these workers with American citizens?

# Information Technology

Application Dependency Mapping
ASP (Application Service Provider)
Backup Systems
Business Process Integration (BPI)
Collaborative Software
Computer Security
Convergence
CRM
Databases
Data Mining
Data Visualization
Denial of Service (DoS) Attacks
Digital Content
Disaster Recovery and Backup
E-Commerce
E-Mail
Enterprise Systems
Extranet
Image Analysis
Information Technology (IT)
Internet
Internet Service Provider (ISP)
Interoperability
Intranets
Management Information Systems (MIS)
Metadata Repository
Network

Records Management
Search Engines
Securing Information Systems and Data
Shopping Cart
Software Compliance
Software Leasing
Storage (data)
TCO (Total Cost of Ownership)
Translation Systems
Unified Messaging
Webcasting
Web Hosting
Web Site
Web Traffic
Year 2000

## Application Dependency Mapping

- What are the dependencies within my application infrastructure?

- Which set of applications and supporting infrastructure work together as a business process to deliver business value?

- Which applications rely on which other applications?

- Which specific database, Web, and application server instance(s) support a particular application?

- Which server(s) does each application rely upon?

- What packaged or custom applications and supporting infrastructure applications are installed, and on what servers are they installed?

- If an infrastructure element malfunctions, which business processes are impacted?

- What recent change in my environment is, or could be, the source of a problem?

- If a change is made to my infrastructure, which applications or business processes will be impacted?

- How does my production environment differ from my development environment?

## ASP (Application Service Provider)

- Whether an application is best implemented as an ASP provided application or service, built in-house, or purchased, generally depends on the same criteria as what would be used for outsourcing a function or process, among them:

- How critical is a system to day-to-day business operations? Does it make better sense to test out a non-core function using the ASP model first before trying out core systems?

- What are the failure recovery requirements for the system?

- How critical are performance requirements for the application?

- How specific is the system's functionality relative to the requirements of other organizations desiring the service?

- What are the cost savings over the development period of an internal system vs. the perceived life of the system?

## Backup Systems

- What backup procedures are in place for the company's network?

- Are all data on all systems backed up?

- Can we verify that this procedure is working properly? Is the recovery process tested annually?

- Does the system call for the removal of a complete backup to an offsite storage facility at least once per month?

- Has the company ever done a complete restore of its network after a system crash? If not, have we verified that capability?

## Business Process Integration (BPI)

- Is IT integrating business processes by migrating to open standards for Business Process Management (BPM) across multiple applications, corporate departments, and business partners, behind the firewall and over the Internet?

## Collaborative Software

- Is the company taking full advantage of collaborative software tools for improving secure business interaction within and across corporate boundaries?

- Are web-based tools implemented that allow the use, viewing, and sharing of sophisticated real-time analytics without requiring advanced analytical skills?

- Does the company's document change control system effectively handle the task of identifying, understanding, and managing changes within documents in multi-authored work environments?

## Computer Security

- How high a priority is information security for the company?

- Who has been the source of a security breach or corporate espionage in the past year?
  [(a) authorized users/employees; (b) unknown; (c) unauthorized users/employees; (d) hackers; (e) terrorists; (f) former employees; (g) contract workers, consultants; (h) suppliers; (i) custom-

ers; (j) competitors; (k) public interest groups; (l) foreign governments]

- What types of security breaches or corporate espionage have occurred within the company in the past year?
  [(a) computer virus; (b) information loss; (c) data/system integrity loss; (d) denial of service; (e) manipulation of software applications; (f) fraud; (g) theft of data/trade secrets; (h) trafficking illegal materials; (i) manipulation of systems programs; (j) Trojan horse; (k) revenue loss]

- How much money has the company lost as a result of breaches or espionage in the past twelve months?

- What is the most important element of the company's information security policy?
  [(a) end-user awareness; (b) business continuity plan; (c) encryption tools; (d) security audits; (e) training IT staff; (f) Year 2000 contingency plan; (g) incident response team]

- What security protection tools does the company use to protect its information systems?
  [(a) virus detection software; (b) firewalls; (c) automated data backup; (d) dial back or secure modems; (e) intrusion detection systems; (f) PC hardware security devices; (g) virtual private networks; (h) security evaluation software; (i) business continuity software; (j) Java/ActiveX controls]

- How often does the company classify sensitive data files and records?

- Are computer users familiar with the security policy? What percentage complies?

- What's the most significant barrier to implementing effective security in the company?
  [(a) lack of time; (b) lack of management support; (c) pace of change; (d) complexity of technology; (e) capital expense; (f) lack of qualified staff; (g) labor expenses]

# Convergence

- What is the company's strategy with respect to the "convergence" of (1) content, (2) communications, (3) commerce, delivered via the three devices (a) T.V., (b) PCs, (c) telephone?

# CRM

- How does the company stack up to ten critical success factors for its CRM implementation?
  [(1) Establish measurable business goals; (2) Align business and IT operations; (3) Get executive support up front; (4) Let business goals drive functionality; (5) Minimize customization by leveraging off-the-shelf functionality; (6) Use trained, experienced consultants; (7) Actively involve end users in solution design; (8) Invest in training to empower users; (9) Use a phased rollout schedule; (10) Measure, monitor, and track.]

- Is the company prepared to utilize software systems that can understand informal written communications and automate appropriate actions?
  [(a) email response management; (b) web self-service; (c) call center agent assist; (d) instant messaging/chat; (e) email productivity; (f) employee relationship management]

# Databases

- Does the company maintain a secured inventory of all its databases of measurable intangible value?

- Does IT have a strategy for managing the data growth on the network and maintaining the necessary performance levels for mission critical systems?

# Data Mining

- Is the company employing data mining techniques to statistically analyze customer transaction data?
- Does the company take advantage of new software tools that allow visualization of the data?

# Data Visualization

- Has the company developed methods to visually analyze key performance data?

# Denial of Service (DoS) Attacks

- How confident is IT with its denial-of-service protection?
- What is the potential for daily revenue loss should an attack lock up one of more production servers?

# Digital Content

- Does the organization have an infrastructure deployed that can quickly and reliably deliver different content formats to different channels?
  audio | graphics | images | multimedia | text | video > call center | iTV | mobile | PC | print | web
- Does company have a Digital Asset Management plan in place such that it can maximize revenue from its digital content?
- Are the necessary systems in place to sell and deliver digital content to any IP-enabled device, including wireless units and personal video recorders, with a variety of payment methods and currencies that allow payments of less than $10?

# Disaster Recovery and Backup

- Is the company's backup system able to conduct incremental backups throughout the workday to minimize data loss in the event of disaster, system failure or corruption?

# E-Commerce

- Is the company considering offering its products/services over the Internet? Can the company be sure of the security of these transactions?

- Does the company currently use (or plan to use) an automated system for order-entry and management?

- Would it help the customer and/or the company if customers could perform their own inventory and price checks, check their order status and place their orders without working through sales reps?

- Could e-commerce save the cost of a comprehensive printed catalog of products?

# E-Mail

- Can the company save a substantial amount of operating costs for infrastructure, software, and personnel by outsourcing its e-mail system operation and maintenance?

- Is IT making full advantage of the collaborative potential of e-mail for most business processes?

# Enterprise Systems

- Does the company have, or plan to have, an integration hub that creates a single point of connectivity for any internal enterprise system to communicate with all external trading partners?

- Does the hub provide channel management, messaging and transaction capabilities for partner integration initiatives with ERP, e-procurement, CRM, financial and any other systems?
- Can the hub provide control and security for all information flow through one single point and perform all data translations, data transformation and session management in real time?

## Extranet

- Is the company's extranet providing customers secure self-service, 24x7 access to account and other information?
- Does the extranet platform provide tools for content management, access control, portals, and user personalization?

## Image Analysis

- Is the company employing state-of-the-art image analysis software systems across a range of applications that would benefit from automation and increased accuracy?
  [(a) security; (b) manufacturing processes; (c) web monitoring]

## Information Technology (IT)

- Is IT deploying a centralized control system on the network to proactively detect and eliminate problems before they happen?
- Does the company have an overall strategic plan for information technology systems (IT)? What are the major changes anticipated in the next 3-5 years?
- In the event of due diligence on the company, can the last three years of annual IT expenditures be broken out?
  [(a) operational; (b) capital; (c) depreciation]
- Is the company's IT comparable or better than the competition?

- Is the company's IT supporting increasing levels of productivity and innovation in the company, or is it a roadblock?

- How do employees rate IT? Management's rating?

- What are IT's priorities?
  [(1) data warehousing; (2) corporate web site; (3) intranet-to-legacy transactions; (4) replacing desktop PCs; (5) e-commerce transactions; (6) network storage; (7) thin-client architecture; (8) supply chain/value chain; (9) replacing portable PCs; (10) component architecture; (11) extranets; (12) OLAP; (13) frame relay over WAN; (14) replacing mainframes]

- In the event of due diligence on the company, is there a readily accessible inventory of hardware and software in use with functional and business descriptions of major systems?

## Internet

- How can the company leverage its investment in technology to take strategic advantage of the Internet? Are we where we should be? Where are the gaps?

- What are our competitors doing on the Internet?

- What security issues must we address?

- Are our Internet efforts building on the corporate vision and the company's core strengths?

- Where will the Internet be in five years, and how are we going to take advantage of this growth?

- How is the Internet changing the behavior of our customer, vendors, and suppliers, and what impacts on the business do we anticipate?

- Does the concept of a virtual community have any relevance to the company?

- How might emerging online intermediaries disrupt the value chain in our industry?

- How are Internet business models impacting traditional business models in our industry?

- Do we have agreement on the Internet's role in our business and is senior management's vision understood by all involved in its implementation?

- Has our Internet team asked customers what they expect from us, determined what our competitors are doing well on the Internet, and analyzed practices in other industries that we can apply for competitive advantage?

- What evidence do we have that our products/services can succeed or require an Internet strategy now or later?

- What is the web-based plan for handling customer requests, customer orders, inventory issues, and other operational issues, and how is this different from our traditional operations?

- Does our Internet team have a balanced marketing and technology perspective, or is it dominated by one or the other?

- What are our projected costs and benefits, including the total organizational investment beyond hardware, software and implementation?

- What are the key timing issues now and in the next 3-5 years with respect to our Internet plans, our business, our industry, and technology?

# Internet Service Provider (ISP)

- Has IT made sure it has evaluated all the relevant factors in its selection of the company's ISP?
  [(a) connection availability; (b) network performance; (c) network capacity; (d) reputation for repair speed; (e) price; (f) service agreements and guarantees; (g) technical support; (h) range

of bandwidth options; (i) staying power in the market (financial stability); (j) ease of start up; (k) security services; (l) online performance monitoring tools; (m) simplicity of billing; (n) brand name]

## Interoperability

- Is IT's EAI (Enterprise Application Integration) strategy including the necessary metadata (context) to provide true interoperability between systems?
  [(a) application interoperability; (b) semantic transformation; (c) ontological mapping]

## Intranets

- Has management considered the cost-effectiveness of a Web-based intranet for inter-company communications and collaboration?

- Is our intranet secure?

- Have we provided multiple levels of user access?

- Are we making full use of the complete inventory of databases within the company?

- Have we planned for current and future storage requirements?

## Management Information Systems (MIS)

- How does the company "mine" its relational database systems for information and trends to be used in the management of the business?

## Metadata Repository

- Has IT built accurate and complete metadata definitions such that data across the enterprise can be re-used transparently in various applications?

- Can users define and create integrated views from the stored metadata definitions?

## Network

- Does the company have a means to maintain a current understanding of all interconnected business applications in spite of the complexity, constant change, and scattered information?

- What backup systems are employed to ensure that the company's network can be fully restored in the event of a complete system crash?

## Records Management

- Has the organization implemented a web-based system that allows us to manage records and documents using the latest bar code, Internet, and relational database technologies? Is it DoD certified?

## Search Engines

- Does the company routinely monitor the ranking of its Web site on the major search engines?

- Is the company's web site optimized to receive high placement in search engine returns?

# Securing Information Systems and Data

- What anti-fraud systems are in place? Can these systems search data stored in multiple, disparate, remote databases and perform real-time risk assessment, decision automation, and non-obvious relationship discovery?

- Has the organization deployed a comprehensive identity management solution that enables secure, centralized management of user rights and privileges to enterprise resources spanning Web-based applications, client-server environments and legacy mainframe systems?

- Has IT physically secured sensitive and critical systems?

- Has IT implemented an anti-virus sensor and response program?

- Has IT developed an assessment program to periodically assess system vulnerabilities?

- Does IT keep operating system and application security patches and repairs up-to-date?

- Has IT developed disaster recovery and business continuity measures?

- Who has organizational responsibility for information security? Have they established administrative standards and procedures for systems security management?

- Has IT created an integrated security architecture?

- When was the last security audit? Results?

# Shopping Cart

- Are the people building the Web site responsive to the needs of the customer?
  [(a) direct link on home page to shopping site; (b) text-only option; (c) specify minimum browser requirement; (d) easy,

intuitive navigation; (e) pre-sale assistance; (f) purchase instructions; (g) product specifications; (h) third-party reviews; (i) features/benefits comparison]

- Have the people building the Web site studied the top e-commerce sites?

## Software Compliance

- Is the company in compliance with all required workstation and network software licenses based on use within the corporation?

## Software Leasing

- Has the company evaluated the cost-effectiveness of leasing certain functional software systems rather than purchasing?

## Storage (data)

- Is IT managing storage as a strategic asset?

## TCO (Total Cost of Ownership)

- Is the company using TCO techniques to prioritize IT investments?

## Translation Systems

- Is the company employing language translation systems so that product documentation, software interfaces, web sites, manuals and marketing collaterals can be localized in many languages quickly and in a highly cost-effective manner?

## Unified Messaging

- Is the company developing plans to integrate unified messaging into its communications infrastructure?
  [Unified messaging allows the user to access voice mail, e-mail, and fax mail in one place through the telephone or computer.]

## Webcasting

- Has the company integrated webcasting across all functions as a cost-effective communications tool?

## Web Hosting

- Does the company's IT staff have the expertise to handle the latest Web applications?

- Can the IT department ensure reliable performance, including the ability to allocate more hardware and Internet bandwidth when traffic volume surges?

- Is the company prepared to budget sufficient funds to set up and operate internal hosting?
  [(a) staff; (b) hardware; (c) software; (d) redundant data centers; (e) security]

## Web Site

- How does the company fully exploit its Web site?

- Is the Web site being used to integrate and increase the speed of information exchange among parties inside and outside the company?

- What impact is the Web site having on the company's overall advertising and promotion program?

- Is the company considering providing multiple language translations of its Web site?

- How robust is the search engine on the company's site? Are customers generally pleased with the relevance of results listings?

## Web Traffic

- Does the company have the necessary Web utilities to deliver highly accurate, real-time information about who is visiting the web sites?

- Can the company gather information regarding web visitors' geographic location (country, state, city, zip code, etc.), the company or organization for which they work, and how they connect to the Internet (Cable, DSL, modem, wireless, etc.)?

## Year 2000

- Does the company continue to test its systems for Y2K compliance?

- Do the company's warranty and maintenance agreements obligate vendors to fix any Y2K problems, and if so, do statutes of limitations and disclaimers limit their effect? Has the company somehow waived claims it might have against such vendors in the future?

# *International Business*

## European Operations

- Will the company's European operations be affected by economic unification in the European community? How is the company preparing for this?

- Does the company feel that its European managers fully understand the changes that are coming in the EU?

- Can the company compete in Europe? What are its strengths, weaknesses, opportunities, and threats in the European market?

## Foreign Imports

- Does the company face noticeable competition from foreign imports?

- What are the company's advantages/disadvantages compared to competing foreign imports?

- What are the applicable U.S. tariff controls to these imports? What is the company's position with respect to these tariffs?

## Foreign Operations

- Does the company employ local managers to run its foreign operations?

## International Business

- What are management's plans for developing international markets for the company's products and services?

- Does the volatility of international markets in general significantly impact the company? How does the company mitigate the impact of volatility?

- What new international markets is management planning to enter? How long will it take realize positive benefits from entering these markets?
  [(a) China; (b) Southeast Asia; (c) Australia; (d) Africa; (e) Canada; (f) Mexico and Central America; (g) Latin America; (h) Europe; (i) Russia]

- Is the company's competitiveness in international markets constrained by any trade restrictions?

- Is compliance to regulations in international markets cost prohibitive?

- Has the pursuit of international markets created inordinately high administrative expenses at the home office?

# *Legal*

Air Quality
Arbitration
Attorney
Bankruptcy
Class-Action Lawsuits
Compliance to Regulations
Contract Administration
Contract Signing Authority
Copyrights
Corporate Records
Enforcement
Environmental Regulations
Escrow Agent
Foreign Corrupt Practices Act
Forms and Agreements
Hazardous Chemical Disposal
Intellectual Property
Lawsuit(s)
Lease Agreements
Legal Information
Legal Proceedings
License Agreements
Negotiating
Nonprofit Organization
North American Free Trade Agreement (NAFTA)
OSHA
Privacy

Questions for Lawyer(s)
Regulations
Regulatory Agencies
Subsidiaries
Trademarks
Tradesecrets
Truth-In-Advertising
Warranty
Waste Production and Disposal
Water Quality

# Air Quality

- Is the air quality of the plant internally and externally in compliance with relevant environmental laws?

- What percentage of the company's revenues is spent to maintain air quality to mandated levels? Is it reasonable or getting out of control?

# Arbitration

- Is the board effectively meeting its responsibility as corporate arbitrator?
  [(a) competing and/or hostile interests; (b) family control; (c) major stockholders]

# Attorney

- What has been the trend in outside attorney fees for the last three years as a percentage of revenue? Is it reasonable?

- Is the company's cost for carrying inside counsel resources reasonable?

# Bankruptcy

- Has the company ever filed, or considered filing, for bankruptcy?
- Are any of the company's vendors in bankruptcy or near bankruptcy?

# Class-Action Lawsuits

- Is the company facing a class-action lawsuit? What are the details?
- Could any large shareholders invoke the "lead plaintiff" provision of the Private Securities Litigation Act naming them a controlling party in the suit?

# Compliance to Regulations

- Is the organization taking advantage of online compliance management systems?
- Does the company have in place an effective ethics and workplace compliance program to guide the actions of employees?
- Has management evaluated the cost-effectiveness of outsourcing the collection, management, and reporting of drug and alcohol testing information across the enterprise?
- Does the program meet the minimum standards set out by the Federal Sentencing Commission?
  [(a) compliance standards and procedures; (b) compliance program oversight; (c) training; (d) monitoring; (e) enforcement and discipline; (f) response and corrective action]
- Is the company in compliance with Federal guidelines for the use and care of animals?

## Contract Administration

- Is contracts administration taking advantage of a secure web-based, centralized, searchable, automated Contracts Management System?
  [(a) integrates multiple contract databases; (b) streamlines contract creation and routing; (c)Automates monitoring of commitments through alerts and notifications; (d) identifies, tracks, invoices and forecasts revenue and expenses more accurately; (e) improves risk management; (f) searches for terms, clauses, and contracts across all contracts; (g) automates license royalties calculations, accounting, and invoicing; (h) integrates with ERP system]

## Contract Signing Authority

- What is the company's policy for contract signing authority? Who is currently authorized to sign contracts?

## Copyrights

- How much protection do copyrights provide?

## Corporate Records

- Where are all the corporate records filed?
- Are backups of all key documents in a secured, disaster-proof location?
- Are the board minutes up-to-date and secure?
- Does the company have a checklist of annual tasks coordinated with 10K filing cycle (and annual report)?

# Enforcement

- Has the company ever been a defendant in any enforcement proceedings by regulatory agencies? Any actions threatened or pending?

# Environmental Regulations

- Have any environmental regulation violations or warnings been given to the company?

- What actions are being taken to resolve the problem(s)? The cost?

- Is the company a candidate for accreditation under the ISO 14000 standards?

# Escrow Agent

- Does the company utilize a third-party escrow agent to safeguard critical systems and propriety software?

- Do customers require this of the company's software products?

- Does the company maintain a current inventory list of what's in escrow? Is it available for review?

# Foreign Corrupt Practices Act

- Is the company in compliance with the Foreign Corrupt Practices Act?

# Forms and Agreements

- Are we reinventing the wheel when it comes to standard forms and agreements, or are we making efficient use of **online resources**?

## Hazardous Chemical Disposal

- Has the company ever had an industrial spill?
- Does the company carry sufficient catastrophe insurance?

## Intellectual Property

- Does the company have an integrated strategy for intellectual property protection? Are all of the company's proprietary rights protected?
- Is intellectual property protection important to this industry?
- How could competitors benefit from a weak intellectual property protection strategy?
- Is it possible for competitors to copy aspects of the company's products without authorization? Is it legal?

## Lawsuits

- What are the top five instigators of class-action lawsuits in the company's industry? Have management and counsel developed proactive measures to mitigate the company's exposure in these areas?
- Is the company currently a party to any lawsuit(s)?
- What is the nature of the suit?
- Does the suit have merit?
- What is the maximum settlement amount? Minimum? Most likely?
- What is the projected settlement date of the suit?

# Lease Agreements

- Does the company have a list of all leases and terms?
  [(a) description; (b) years remaining; (c) min./max. annual payment; (d) escalations; (e) adjustments; (f) renewals; (g) options to purchase.]

- Does the company have a list of all capital lease payments due for the next three years, and the imputed interest to derive the present value of such future lease payments?

# Legal Information

- In the event of due diligence on the company, is all important legal information reasonably accessible in one location?
  [(a) leases; (b) employment contracts; (c) independent contractor contracts; (d) union contracts; (e) sales contracts; (f) pension plans; (g) benefit plans (profit sharing, post-retirement); (h) deferred compensation agreements; (i) article of incorporation for all legal entities in the corporation; (j) by-laws; (k) short and long-term debt agreements; (l) product catalogs; (m) list of intellectual property (patents, trademarks, copyrights); (n) licenses and royalty agreements; (o) franchise agreements; (p) credit agreements; (q) all filings with Federal agencies in the last five years; (r) all outstanding proposals affecting existing contracts; (s) maintenance contracts]

# Legal Proceedings

- Has the company been involved in any significant litigation in the past three years?

- Are there any actions, lawsuits, proceedings pending or threatened against the company or any officers and directors? Is the company at risk?
  [(a) wage and hour law; (b) hiring practice regulation; (c) occupational safety laws; (d) licensing laws; (e) environmental laws]

- Are there any legal threats in the industry at large that could indirectly or directly impact the company?

## License Agreements

- Are the company's license agreements effective revenue generators?

## Negotiating

- Have the company's key negotiators been trained in professional negotiation strategies and tactics?

## Nonprofit Organization

- Is the organization taking advantage of web-based tools tailored for nonprofits?

## North American Free Trade Agreement (NAFTA)

- Has the company been able to capitalize on NAFTA? How?

## OSHA

- What are the troublesome occupational hazards for the company?
- What has the company's record been with past OSHA inspections? Any fines?
- Has the company corrected all violations?

## Privacy

- Does the company have in place a privacy compliance program to mitigate risk exposure in this area?

[(a) damage to the organization's reputation and business relationships; (b) charges of deceptive business practices; (c) customer and employee distrust; (d) denial of consent to use personal information for business purposes; (e) lost business, profits and market share; (f) legal liability and industry sanctions]

- What personal information about customers and employees does the organization collect and retain?

- What personal information is used in carrying out business, for example, in sales, marketing, fundraising and customer relations?

- What personal information is obtained from, or disclosed to, affiliates or third parties, for example, in payroll outsourcing?

- What is the impact of the Personal Information Protection and Electronic Documents Act (PIPEDA) and/or international privacy requirements, on the organization (a legal interpretation may be required)?

- How does the organization's business plan address the privacy of personal information?

- To what degree is senior management actively involved in the development, implementation and/or promotion of privacy measures within the organization?

- Has the organization assigned someone (for example, a Chief Privacy Officer) the responsibility for compliance with privacy legislation?

- Has the designated privacy officer been given clear authority to oversee the organization's information handling practices?

- Are adequate resources available for developing, implementing and maintaining a privacy compliance system?

- What privacy policies has the organization established with respect to the collection, use, disclosure and retention of personal information?

- How are the policies and procedures for managing personal information communicated to employees?

- How are employees with access to personal information trained in privacy protection?

- Are the appropriate forms and documents required by the system fully developed?

- To comply with the organization's established privacy policies, what specific objectives have been established?

- What are the consequences of not meeting the specific privacy objectives?

- To what extent have appropriate control measures been identified and implemented?

- How is the effectiveness of the privacy control measures monitored and reported?

- What mechanisms are in place to deal effectively with failures to properly apply the organization's established privacy policies and procedures?

- How would the organization benefit from a comprehensive assessment of the risks, controls and business disclosures associated with personal information privacy?

- Has the organization considered the value-added services available from an independent assurance practitioner with respect to both offline and online privacy?

## Questions for Lawyer(s)

- Are there any suits against the company outstanding?

- Are there any potential suits against the company?

- Has the company filed suits against others that are still open? Does the company plan to file a suit(s) against others?

- Are there any product liability suits or problems?

- Are there any patent suits or problems?

- Are there any union suits or problems?

- What is your evaluation of management?

- Is management listening to your best advice?

# Regulations

- What are the major regulatory bodies which control this industry?

- Is there a trend towards more government regulation in this industry?

# Regulatory Agencies

- Has the company experienced any regulatory problems or complaints within the past two years with any local, state, or federal agency? Any action threatened or pending?

- Is the company in compliance with all federal, state and local laws?

# Subsidiaries

- Are there any conditions which are restricting contribution payments from subsidiaries to the parent company?

- Has the company followed through on all promises and performance guarantees to its subsidiaries?

# Trademarks

- Does the company have a strategy and procedures for trademark protection where it makes sense?

- Is trademarking a cost-effective strategy for the company's products and services?

# Tradesecrets

- What products ands processes are trade secreted within the company?

- What is the risk to the company should these trade secrets get in the hands of competitors?

# Truth-In-Advertising

- Are there any problems or claims with respect to truth-in-advertising?

# Warranty

- What types of failures have been most likely to trigger claims? Do we clearly understand the Federal guidelines?

- Can these claims be avoided without resorting to warranty?

- Does the warranty apply passively to all sales, or is the customer required to apply or qualify for warranty coverage? What are the requirements?

- What percentage of annual revenues is spent to fulfill the company's warranty obligations?

- How much warranty reserve does the company maintain? Is it adequate?

- Does the warranty appeal to the customer? Does market research support this?

- Has the company implemented an online warranty management system to automate and optimize this function, and therefore reduce costs?

## Waste Production and Disposal

- How much and what kinds of scrap or waste are generated by the production process?

- How is waste/scrap disposed?

- Is the company in compliance with environment control regulations for each type of waste or scrap byproduct?

- Are there any major capital requirements needed in the future to maintain compliance? Has the company allocated funds in the long-term financial plan?

## Water Quality

- Is the water quality of the plant internally and externally in compliance with relevant environmental laws?

- What percentage of the company's revenues does it spend to maintain water quality to mandated levels? Is it reasonable or getting out of control?

# Management & Best Practices

Benchmarking
Business Process Reengineering
CEO
CEO Performance Evaluation
CEO Succession
Consultants
Entrepreneurship
Excellence
Executive Compensation
Executive Perks
Heir-Apparent
Inside Candidates
Interim CEO
Management
Management Development Program
Management Reports
Outsourcing
Politics
Power
Professional Advisers
Turnaround

## Benchmarking

- What key performance measures have been benchmarked in the company?

- How does the company perform to these benchmarks?

# Business Process Reengineering

- Does the company have a system in place that can correlate and map low-level system events to high-level business views to detect and diagnose business performance problems at the functional level?

- What are our major business processes?

- Do the company's collaborative systems archive projects and processes so they can be reused as best practices?

- How do these processes interface with customer and supplier processes?

- What are our strategic, value-adding processes?

- Which processes should we reengineer within three months, six months, one year, and subsequently?

- What organizations and jobs are involved in the processes? What pieces of work are done by each job?

- What policies apply to the performance of the processes? In which piece of work does each policy apply?

- What technology is used in the processes? In which piece of the work is the technology used?

- How do we identify processes that are conducive to redesign? [(a) High customer requirement, but low performance (customers complain); (b) Some things just take too long; (c) High cost of poor quality (errors, rework, mistakes, scrap); (d) The company throws people at the problem, but things don't get better; (e) High internal frustration factor and low morale; (f) Process spans several functions and there is finger pointing and blaming; (g) Process is not being measured, high variability in output or results; (h) Excessive information exchange, data redundancy, and re-keying of data; (i) Inventory, buffers, and other assets sitting idle; (j) High ratio of checking and control to value adding;

(k) Complexity, exceptions, and special cases; (l) No one is responsible for the process.]

# CEO

- When's the last time our CEO rolled up his or her sleeves and worked alongside employees? Is s/he in touch with "the floor"? Does s/he have employees' respect?

## CEO Performance Evaluation

- Does the chairman (board) annually evaluate the CEO?

- What behaviors and competencies are desired in the CEO to lead the company today and into the future? Are they continually altered to fit the unique technical and industry requirements arising in the marketplace?
  [(a) performance as measured against current objectives; (b) progress towards strategic objectives; (c) business conduct and integrity; (d) match between CEO competencies and company's needs, current and future; (e) leadership abilities, response from staff; (f) physical and psychological fitness; (g) quality of relationships with the board]

- Does the board require the CEO to complete a self-evaluation?

- Has the board benchmarked the strategic performance of CEOs at peer companies?

- Is the board responsive to the concerns of shareholders about the effectiveness and responsiveness of management?

- Is the incumbent CEO in good health?

- On what grounds is the board considering firing the CEO?
  [(a) poor company performance; (b) strategic disagreement with the board; (c) personality clashes; (d) consolidation of control due to merger; (e) unwillingness of CEO to comply with a

board mandate; (f) personal problems; (g) illegal/improper behavior]

# CEO Succession

- Is the compensation committee responsible for CEO succession, or has a special committee been formed for this function?

- Does the board have a plan for an interim CEO in the event of a sudden and unexpected departure or death of the CEO? [(a) insider; (b) director; (c) independent interim manager]

- Is competition among internal candidates getting out of hand?

- Is the incumbent CEO the right leader at the right time?

- Does the board have a healthy collaboration with the incumbent CEO in the succession process?

- Has the board established clear performance benchmarks and an exit timetable for the incumbent CEO?

- Is the incumbent CEO attracting, hiring, and developing key employees worthy of succession candidacy? Is there a turnover problem with top management candidates?

- Does the incumbent CEO restrict access by the board to top management? Are executive session meetings of the outside directors discouraged by the CEO?

- Should the board consider removing the incumbent CEO from the board?

- Is the board developing and maintaining a familiarity with top succession candidates within and external to the company?

- Is retirement of the incumbent CEO being delayed by lack of a successor?

- For the incumbent CEO close to retirement, has the board structured a compensation package heavily weighted towards stock options vesting after retirement giving him/her incentive to cooperate with a successful transition?

## Consultants

- In what areas does the company find it cost-effective to use outside consultants?

## Entrepreneurship

- Has the company considered experimenting with an entrepreneur-in-residence program to stimulate and encourage internal entrepreneurial forces?

## Excellence

- Are we a great company? If not, do we know what it will take and are we pursuing a plan to get there?

## Executive Compensation

- In general, are executive compensation packages reflective of individual performance?
- Are executive compensation packages competitive with others in the industry?
- Are compensation packages effective in attracting and retaining talented individuals?

## Executive Perks

- At a minimum, is the company matching the most common perqs provided to CEOs and key executives?
  [(a) physical exams; (b) financial counseling; (c) company car; (d) income tax preparation; (e) communications equipment]

# Heir-Apparent

- Has the incumbent CEO hand-picked a successor who is intentionally weak?
- Has the board challenged the heir-apparent to be compared against external candidates?
- Has the board been able to observe and evaluate the heir-apparent in representative trial assignments?

# Inside Candidates

- Is the board comparing internal leadership candidates against their peers in outside peer companies?

# Interim CEO

- Does the board have at least one member with the qualifications to serve as interim CEO in the event of an emergency?
- Does it make more sense to consider an interim CEO and/or CFO at this stage, before filling these positions with full-time long-term candidates?

# Management

- What are the ages of the executive management team?
- Has the current management team worked together in the past?
- Has there been a consultant's evaluation/report on management?
- What are the gaps in the present management structure? Are there plans in place to close the gaps?
- Has any member of the management team violated any major laws in the past twenty years?

- How are the corporate officers officially registered?

## Management Development Program

- Does the company have in place a formal management development program?

## Management Reports

- What financial reports are provided to the CEO and the top management?
- Are reports distributed in time to be useful? Are they accurate?
- Are performance reports prepared for all major areas of accountability?
- Do these reports relate actual performance to plans and budgets?
- Is adequate information being provided to manage effectively and make informed decisions?
- In terms of centralized reporting, does the interface between subsidiaries, divisions, and departments with corporate headquarters work smoothly?
- Is the company preparing to meet the new International Accounting Standards necessary to operate in EU markets?

## Outsourcing

- Is outsourcing an appropriate and effective strategy to keep the company as lean as possible and reduce working capital requirements to a minimum?
- What functions are being considered for outsourcing? What are the anticipated benefits and cost reductions?

# Politics

- Has the company been affected by changes in politics at the local, state, and national level?

- Does the company manage its political affairs and involvement in a manner that is appropriate and legal?
  [(a) Campaign contributions; (b) Lobbying; (c) Political Action Committees (PACs)]

# Power

- How is power consolidated in the company?

- Are directors careful to not get involved in the internal politics of the company?

# Professional Advisers

- Does the company rely heavily on outside professional advisers? Is the rate of spending reasonable?

# Turnaround

- Does the board need to consider an outside turnaround specialist to manage the current crisis in the company?

# Manufacturing & Distribution

Automation
Dealers
Demand-Chain Management
Distribution
Excess Capacity
Finished Goods
Franchising
ISO Standards
Just-In-Time Delivery
Logistics
Manufacturing Capacity
Manufacturing Equipment
Manufacturing Facilities
Manufacturing Personnel
Manufacturing Flow and Processes
Manufacturing Ratios
Ocean Shipping
Purchasing
Quality Management Program
Questions for Suppliers
Raw Materials
Receiving
Recycling
Scrap
Service Supply Chain
Shipping
Sourcing

Subcontract Work
Suppliers
Supply-Chain Management
Work in Progress
Workflow Automation

## Automation

- How much automation exists within each major manufacturing operation?

- How much additional automation can be implemented in the manufacturing operations?

- What would the capital requirements be?

- What would be the effects on production?
  [(a) costs; (b) labor utilization; (c) labor content of costs; (d) production flexibility]

- To what extent are finished products and components standardized?

## Dealers

- Has the company maximized its use of the Web in its dealership strategy?

- Does the company have an effective online dealership locator?

## Demand-Chain Management

- Does the company's merchandising planning systems make it possible to quickly test out the viability of any scenario and fully understand the financial impacts and other implications of a variety of decisions?

- Does the system make it possible to visually simulate an exact 3-D replication of the store shelf and the products in order to get a true preview of the shelf schematic?

- Does the system allow for web-based collaboration with internal and external partners?

- Are we performing cluster analysis to optimize our merchandising decisions?

- Is the company using a web-based demand analytics system to get a clear view of product movement through all the distribution channels? What are the benefits?
[(a) optimize product mix; (b) identify revenue opportunities; (c) reduce channel inventory buffers and WIP; (d) increase partner satisfaction; (e) enhance forecast accuracy; (f) reduce operating costs]

## Distribution

- How many distributors does the company use?
- What is the geographical distribution of distributors?
- What is the average number of salesman per distributor?
- What percentage of distributors' sales are company products?
- How are distributors selected?
[(a) sales force; (b) customer network; (c) financial stability; (d) reputation]
- What is the compensation arrangement with distributors? Is the compensation arrangement competitive with their other product lines?
- What credit terms are extended to the distributor?
- Does the distributor purchase products from the company or simply take a commission on sales?
- How much company support is provided to distributors?

- How does the company insure a consistent sales approach among its distributors?
- What is the availability of qualified distributors?
- How does the company evaluate the cost-effectiveness of distributors vs. a direct sales force?

## Excess Capacity

- Where does excess capacity exist in the corporation? [(a) employees; (b) equipment; (c) buildings]

## Finished Goods

- What happens to finished goods that do not pass quality tests?

## Franchising

- Has the company evaluated the cost-effectiveness of franchising as a business model for distributing its products and services?

## ISO Standards

- Has any customer or governing body in any of the company's markets mandated a requirement that the company be ISO 9000 registered?

## Just-In-Time Delivery

- How does the company monitor and evaluate the performance and impact of its just-in-time delivery?

# Logistics

- Is the company deriving the full benefits of global transportation and logistics software which enables the company to move goods through the supply chain, across all modes and geographies, as a single, integrated, collaborative process?
  [(a) Deliver freight at lower cost; (b) Reduce inventory and shorten cycle times; (c) Optimize supply chain performance; (d) Gain competitive advantage with improved customer service and satisfaction; (e) Position the business for growth]

# Manufacturing Capacity

- At what percentage of capacity is the company operating?

- What is the minimum feasible increment in the expansion of production capacity?

- What is the incremental sales volume required to break even on the minimum feasible incremental production capacity?

- How does the company's utilization of production capacity compare with its competitors?

# Manufacturing Equipment

- How much downtime does the company experience with equipment?

- Is there a backup plan to every critical piece of production equipment in case of shutdown?

- Are replacement parts readily available?

- Is the equipment generally in good operating condition?

- Is the company's equipment comparable, if not superior, to the age and sophistication of competitors' equipment?

- Is any of the production equipment highly specialized or custom-made?

## Manufacturing Facilities

- How old is the existing plant(s)?
- What condition is the plant(s) in?
- Are the annual maintenance and repair costs reasonable?
- Is there a formal preventive maintenance program in effect?
- What is the remaining useful life of the plant(s)?
- Is the production capacity of the plant(s) adequate? Is the plant(s) operating at capacity?
- What is the rationale for the current distribution of production capacity across plant sites?
  [(a) customer distribution; (b) shipment requirements; (c) raw material supply; (d) labor supply]
- How much flexibility is there to shift production between plants?
- What is the replacement value of the plant(s)?
- What is the book value of the plant(s)?
- What is the liquidation value of the plant(s)?
- Is there adequate insurance coverage on the plant(s) to cover replacement value?
- Have there been any recent appraisals?

## Manufacturing Personnel

- How is productivity measured?
- How competitive are the company's manufacturing wage rates?

- Are any incentive plans in effect?

- Is the turnover rate acceptable for manufacturing personnel?

- Are there backup personnel for each position?

- What are the top manufacturing personnel problems?

- Has the company experienced any Equal Employment Opportunity (EEO) problems in the last twelve months?

## Manufacturing Flow and Processes

- How is the weekly/monthly production schedule established?

- What is the length of each production cycle?

- Is the production flow generally efficient?

- Are there any bottlenecks that are a problem in any of the production segments?

- Has production been completely stopped in the last year? What are the chances this could happen again, and why?

- How much flexibility exists to shift production between plants?

- Can the company increase throughput in any of the production segments?

- How does in-line vs. batch processing compare?

- How do the company's production processes benchmark with competitors?

- What is the procedure for identifying and reporting production problems?

- How many quality test points are there in the production process?

# Manufacturing Ratios

- How do the company's ratios compare with industry norms?

- What is the three-year trend in these ratios?

- Employee Productivity = [(Direct labor hours) / (Units produced)] hours/unit

- Labor Content = [($Labor costs) / ($Total production costs)] %

- Material Content = [($Material costs) / ($Total production costs] %

- Idle Time = [(Total idle time hours) / (Total available labor hours)] %

- Scheduling Efficiency = [(Overtime hours) / (Total hours worked)] %

- Machine Utilization = [(Production machine hours) / (Total available hours)] %

- Scrap Rate = [(# units scrapped) / (Total units produced)] %

# Ocean Shipping

- How will the Ocean Shipping Reform Act affect the company?

# Purchasing

- Has the company's web-based procurement system achieved CMM Level 2 Certification? Have we been audited by OCC (if that is relevant)? What were the results?

- Do the company's database systems allow purchasing to aggregate spending across business lines and geographies?

- Are there any inventory items for which less than two suppliers are available?

- Does the company feel it has the best prices and credit terms achievable from its major suppliers?

- Are we exploiting the buying power of a "reverse auction pool" of businesses to negotiate corporate rates for core services from brand-name providers?

- How are product specifications developed for items purchased?

- Is the company's purchase requisition/approval procedure tight or loose? Is there a written procedure? What would an external audit conclude?

## Quality Management Program

- Does the company have a quality manual?

- What procedures does the company have for testing incoming raw materials and component parts? What are the quality standards for each component and material? What happens to parts or shipments that do not meet quality standards?

- What is the average failure rate for products in final test?

- What has been the company's experience with each supplier of key components?

- Is the company ISO 9000 certified?

- Does the company employ any full-time quality management staff?

- When was the last external audit?

- How complete and accurate are the quality records?

## Questions for Suppliers

- Do you anticipate any shortages in the items you supply to the company?

- How promptly are you paid by the company? Is it ever a problem?
- What do you like about the company?
- How would you describe your relationship with the company?
- How are you treated as a supplier?
- Will you continue to supply the company?

# Raw Materials

- What are the principal materials used in manufacturing each product?
- What is the company's physical proximity to raw material sources?
- How are raw materials transported?
- How would a slowdown in transportation services affect the company's operations?
- Are any of the raw materials used by the company dependent on a harvest each year? What percentage?
- How does the company control the risks associated with the price fluctuation of these materials?
- What procedures does the company have for testing incoming raw materials?

# Receiving

- Is there a written procedure for receiving goods and services?
- Who is authorized to sign receiving tickets?
- What system is in place to reduce the possibility of internal theft?

# Recycling

- Can finished goods that fail quality tests be recycled?

# Scrap

- What are the various types and sources of scrap?
- How is scrap disposed?

# Service Supply Chain

- Has the company implemented a web-based **service parts planning system** to optimize the balance between supply chain costs and customer availability? Are we tracking the gains against a baseline?
  [(a) Inventory investment reduction; (b) Annual expediting costs; (c) Global availability improvement; (d) Significant increase in planner and field engineer productivity; (e) Increased product sales due to improved service]

# Shipping

- Is there a written procedure(s) for shipping?
- How does accounting confirm what goods are shipped?
- How does the company confirm that the customer received the goods?
- What systems are in place to prevent theft?

# Sourcing

- What stage of development has the company achieved with the implementation and use of e-sourcing tools and strategies?

- Can the company implement and master systems a module at a time?

## Subcontract Work

- What is the list of all work-for-hire contracts?
- Are there any problems with subcontracted work?
- Are there multiple alternative subcontractors for these services?
- Are there any critical parts/services from one subcontractor?

## Suppliers

- Has the company set up an electronic payment and remittance system to speed transactions and reduce costs?
- Do the company's database systems make it easy to identify the best and worst suppliers?
- How are suppliers selected?
  [(a) quality; (b) timeliness; (c) price; (d) other]
- Does the company maintain an "Approved Vendors List"?
- How often do suppliers fail to deliver on time?
- What are the chances of a serious interruption in delivery from a key supplier?
- Are any suppliers near bankruptcy? What effect on production schedules has this had?
- Are there any unsatisfactory relationships with key suppliers?
- Are the company's major suppliers in stable industries? In the future?
- Are any of these key suppliers vertically integrating such that they look more like competitors?

- Does the company have an over dependence on one or a few key suppliers? What would be the delay and cost impact if the company were to lose one of its key suppliers?

- Are the company's trade payables current?

- Is the company considering developing information system linkages (extranet) with its key suppliers?
  [(a) production; (b) inventory; (c) sales; (d) specifications; (e) scheduling]

## Supply-Chain Management

- Does the company have a methodology (and systems) in place to mitigate risks and volatility in its sourcing agreements?

## Work in Progress

- How are work-in-progress inventory levels monitored?

- When was work-in-progress inventory last evaluated?

- How are work-in-progress inventory adjustments accounted for?

## Workflow Automation

- Has the company modeled its workflow processes?

- What software systems are in place to optimize the workflow model within the company?

# *Marketing*

Advertising and Promotion
Barriers to Entry
Brand Identity and Loyalty
Business Cycles
Business Intelligence
Business Plans
Business Writing
Buying Decisions
Competition
Competitive Threats
Consolidation
Corporate Image
Customer Acquisition
Customer Demand
Customer Dependence
Customer Feedback
Customer Profile
Customer Satisfaction
Demographics
Economic Conditions
Editorial Coverage
Gap Analysis
Globalization
Industry Trends
Installed Base
Lease Pricing
Market Definition

Market Research
Market Share
Market Trends
Outdoor Advertising
Permission Marketing
Pricing
Pricing Management
Promotion
Publications
Questions for Advertising Agency
Radio
Telephone Interviews (surveys)
Trade Periodicals
Writing for the Web

## Advertising and Promotion

- What percentage of revenues is required to competitively advertise and promote the company's products?

- What are the top five most effective marketing and promotional strategies?

- How effectively does marketing solicit and integrate the advertising ideas from other divisions of the company?

- How does the company evaluate the effectiveness of advertising and promotional programs?

## Barriers to Entry

- Is this an easy market to enter?

- What are the barriers to entry?

# Brand Identity and Loyalty

- What is the degree of brand loyalty among customers?
- How does the company measure brand loyalty?
- What strategies are employed to "lock in" brand loyalty?
- What would be required to persuade users of competitive products to switch? What are the costs to the customer to switch?

# Business Cycles

- What are the major drivers to the key product/company business cycles?
- Can the company reliably predict a cycle upturn or downturn?
- Are the company's operations significantly affected by weather patterns?
- Are we comparing leading domestic indicators against external events to determine the expected impact on our business?

# Business Intelligence

- Are the company's systems extensible to meet today's data demands, and scalable to meet tomorrow's?
- Does the company have database tools that allow users complete analysis, complete control of data, and the flexibility to change at any time?
- Does the company have reliable alternatives to closed mainframes that are easy to manage, maintain, and that interoperate with multiple business applications?
- Is management capable of decision-making and reaction to market change based on accurate, real-time intelligence from multiple data points?

- Are employees empowered to independently access and analyze enterprise data and access that data anywhere, on any device?

- Does the company have the ability to anticipate customer needs through thorough knowledge of their buying history and habits?

- Does the company have the ability to get customers the information they need, and information in the hands of those with the most customer contact?

- Can the company minimize costs and maximize resources through integration with legacy systems?

- Can the company integrate data mining and analysis tools in the same box to facilitate rapid deployment?

- Can the company leverage familiar tools to simplify training, application creation, and thus increase time to benefit?

- Are the company's systems easy to integrate, deploy, manage and use?

- Does management have the ability to identify opportunities by merging and analyzing the growing mass of information from multiple data points?

- What solution provider is the company considering to help plan, design, and deploy business intelligence?

## Business Plans

- Is management disciplined about preparing business plans when evaluating any new major business initiative?

## Business Writing

- Does the company have an internal "Manual of Style"?

## Buying Decisions

- Is the company's Web site optimized to assist the customer through the buying decision process as quickly and easily as possible?
- What are the typical stages in the buying decision?
- What is the typical length of a buying decision?
- What are the driving criteria in the buying decision? [(a) credit terms; (b) customer service; (c) delivery speed; (d) pricing (e) product features; (f) reputation; (g) sales rep relationships]
- Are buying decisions affected by advertising and promotion?
- What is the customer's sensitivity to price?

## Competition

- Who are the company's five top competitors?
- How would you rate their financial strength?
- What is their percentage of market share?
- How much does the company know about competitors' management and business in general?
- Does the company monitor the annual reports of its competitors?
- What does a competitor comparative analysis show about our company's market, product position, and pricing?
- Are there any expected new entries to the market?
- Has management developed defensive and offensive strategies to deal with new competing products and services?
- How will this impact sales and profits?

- Has increased global competition brought in new international competitors?
- What systems are in place to collect competitor intelligence?

## Competitive Threats

- Is the company in danger of being leap-frogged by the emerging e-business capabilities of a competitor?

## Consolidation

- Has there been any consolidation in the industry?
- How does consolidation affect the company?

## Corporate Image

- What does the company do to insure a consistent corporate image?
  [(a) marketing; (b) advertising; (c) sales; (d)products]

## Customer Acquisition

- Is sales taking advantage of **web-based systems** to optimize and accelerate the customer acquisition process?
  [(a) demand generation; (b) sales lead qualification; (c) sales lead management; (d) closed loop reporting]

## Customer Demand

- Will the industry be able to meet demand now and in the future?
- What product(s) don't we have that are in need or would complete our current product line?

# Customer Dependence

- Is the company dependent on a few key customers?

- What percentage of projected sales is represented by these key customers?

- Are any of these customers in financial trouble? Does anyone in the company routinely monitor this?

- Does the company have any contracts or special arrangements with key customers?

- Has the company lost any major customers in the past two years? Is the company about to lose a major customer?

- Have any new major customers been added through increased global trade?

# Customer Feedback

- In what ways does the company gather customer feedback?

- How have customers rated the company and its products in the past? Currently?

# Customer Profile

- Does the company maintain a list of its top ten customers by sales volume?

- Why does the customer buy the company's products and services?

- What are the driving trends of the typical customer?

## Customer Satisfaction

- Can the company continuously measure website users' satisfaction and future behaviors, such as the likelihood to return to the site or refer the site to others?

## Demographics

- What is the demographic breakout of the company's customer base?
  [(a) geography; (b) gender; (c) income; (d) occupation; (e) age]

## Economic Conditions

- To what degree is the company influenced by broad economic conditions?
  [(a) trade balance; (b) housing starts; (c) unemployment; (d) consumer price index; (e) money supply, M2]

- Does the company track these indicators?

- What is the current economic situation as it affects the company? Projected?

## Editorial Coverage

- Are we maximizing the quality and scope of editorial coverage we promote to editors?

## Gap Analysis

- Does the company conduct a gap analysis on an annual or semi-annual basis to evaluate business processes against system functionality?

# Globalization

- How effectively is the company meeting the challenges of globalizing its operations?
  [(a) workable global structure; (b) unifying employees; (c) attracting and retaining managers with advanced cultural, linguistic, and personal skills; (d) embracing cultural diversity]

- Is it more appropriate and feasible for the company to organize its global operations by product vs. geography?

# Industry Trends

- What are the major trade publications and trade associations that report events and make analyses of this industry and the companies that compete in this industry?

- Does the company keep a current list of all industry analysts and experts?

- What are the industry analysts and experts generally reporting about the industry and the company's competitive position in the industry?

- Is the company aware of those venture capitalists and other capital sources that have invested in this industry?

- Is the industry in or entering a trend of merger and acquisitions?

- Are there any business failures in the industry? Why?

- Are companies concentrated in any particular way?
  [(a) geography; (b) product line; (c) pricing level; (d) customer type]

- Does this industry have a high dependence on key customers?

- What is the industry growth rate?

- What are the factors affecting future growth of the industry?

# Installed Base

- What is the geographic distribution of the installed based of customers?
- What is the 3-year trend in growth of the installed base?

# Lease Pricing

- What percentage of sales are leases?
- What is the length of a typical lease?
- What percentage are full payout leases?
- Does the company have any third-party leasing agreements at present?

# Market Definition

- How big is the overall market?
- What percentage is domestic vs. international?
- What has been the overall market growth rate for the last five years?
- What has been the market growth rate by product for the last five years?
- What is the geographic distribution of the market?
  [by (a) customer location; (b) sales volume; (c) customer type]
- How will that geographic distribution change in the next five years?
- Is the market typically a seasonal or cyclical one?

## Market Research

- Is the company developing Web-based research techniques to supplement traditional mail and phone surveys?

## Market Share

- What is the company's share of the market? Trend for the last five years?
- What are management's plans to increase market share?

## Market Trends

- Will the concentration in market share change in the next five years?
- Will price competition increase in the next five years?

## Outdoor Advertising

- Is outdoor advertising a cost-effective tactic for the company's products and services?

## Permission Marketing

- Is the organization exploiting the full power of e-mail permission marketing?
- Are e-campaigns making use of incentive offers to accelerate opt-ins and build customer relationships?
- Is the company exploiting mobile marketing to deliver targeted marketing campaigns to any wireless device?

# Pricing

- How is pricing strategy developed in the company?
- What are the factors that affect pricing strategy?
  [(a) cost-of-goods sold; (b) overhead; (c) competitors' pricing; (d) past pricing trend; (e) customer sensitivity to price; (f) volume; (g) "market-will-bear" pricing]
- What has been the price trend for the past five years?
- What is the price trend for the next five years?
- Will price competition increase in the next five years?
- Is there a price leader in the industry? If it's not the company, why?
- Do salespeople (and others) have the approval to sell products at a price that differs from the approved price list?
- Are prices reviewed / adjusted each year?
- Can cost increases generally be passed on to the customer?

# Pricing Management

- Do we have a good understanding of how our customers react to price changes or discounting policies?
- Have we correctly segmented our customers when it comes to pricing and discounting?
- Do we provide our sales channels clear discounting guidelines and targets?
- Do our sales people offer discounts outside of margin guidelines?
- Can we quickly adapt to market changes to achieve short-term objectives without sacrificing margin or damaging long-term growth?

- Do we have real-time visibility into profit performance by channel, product, and customer segment?
- Are we able to quickly sense and respond to emerging opportunities and competitive threats as they arise?
- Is our pricing and promotion strategy driven only by costs and competition, or more by our customers?

## Promotion

- Is the company taking advantage of web-based resources that can provide real-time feedback on the performance of promotional tactics?

## Publications

- Does the company sponsor subscriptions to key board resource publications for directors?

## Questions for Advertising Agency

- How long have you been the advertising agency?
- What is the company's annual advertising budget?
- Does the company pay its bills on time? Have you ever had to contact the company for failing to pay?
- Is the company a good customer?
- Is management listening to your best advice?

## Radio

- Is radio a cost-effective marketing channel for our business? If so, are we optimizing its use?

## Telephone Interviews (surveys)

- Has marketing considered outsourcing certain research studies to telephone survey specialists?

## Trade Periodicals

- How does the company utilize the top three trade periodicals?

## Writing for the Web

- Does the company have a content strategy that recognizes the different requirements and limitations of an online environment?

- Is the content carefully checked, edited, and refreshed on an appropriate cycle?

# *Products & Services*

Business Models
Learning-Driven Commerce
New Product Assessment
New Products
Product Differentiation
Product Features
Product Liability
Product Life Cycle
Product Profitability
Product Reliability
Product Returns
Product Value (Utility)
Project Profitability
Retail
Service Features
Service Life Cycle
Service Profitability
Service Value/Utility
Subscription Services

## Business Models

- Does the company have a clear understanding of its business (profit) model for each product? Should other models be considered?

## Learning-Driven Commerce

- Is the company taking advantage of the Internet to integrate an online learning center within its e-commerce platform to increase customer loyalty and ultimately sales?

## New Product Assessment

- What market characteristics demonstrate attractiveness for the new product opportunity?
  [(a) size; (b) growth; (c) stage in market life cycle; (d) number of potential customers; (e) intensity of competition; (f) number of competitors; (g) extent of loyalty to existing offerings; (h) satisfaction with existing offerings; (i) importance of government regulations, legislation, etc.]

- What risks are associated with developing and delivering the new product or service?
  [(a) degree of innovation required; (b) level of technology; (c) cost/profitability; (d) technical complexity; (e) origin of idea; (f) clarity of initial specifications; (g) defensive vs. offensive positioning; (h) learning needed by company for market entry]

- What is the adequacy of the company's resources to successfully develop and commercialize this new product idea?
  [(a) financial skills; (b) R&D skills; (c) engineering skills; (d) marketing research skills; (e) management skills; (f) production resources; (g) sales force, distribution, service; (h) advertising and promotion]

- What are the competitive advantages of the new product or service?
  [(a) uniqueness of features/attributes; (b) ability to satisfy customer needs; (c) ability to reduce customer costs; (d) additional functionality; (e) quality; (f) price; (g) timing of entry]

# New Products

- Have new products/services achieved expected levels of profit-ability?

- What are management's short-term (1 year) and long-term (5 years) new product/service plans?

# Product Differentiation

- Does management clearly understand the positioning of its products and services in the marketplace?
[(a) price; (b) performance; (c) features]

# Product Features

- What are the top five features of this product(s)?

- What could be considered proprietary features?

- Have there been any reviews / comparisons of the product(s)?

- What is the market positioning strategy for each product?

- Is the company using a Web-based system to gather customer feedback and iteratively test design options and preferences?

# Product Liability

- What type of coverage, in what amounts, of product liability insurance does the company carry?

- Are there any product liability claims?

# Product Life Cycle

- At what stage in the product life cycle is each of the company's core products?

## Product Profitability

- What is the sales volume for each product?
- What is the profitability (gross margin) of each product?
- Is there a relationship between a product's sales/profitability ranking and incentives for salespeople?

## Product Reliability

- What is the mean time to failure for each product?
- How does the company rank the reliability of each product?
- How sensitive is the customer to product quality?

## Product Returns

- Is the company deploying a system that makes product returns easy and efficient for the customer?

## Product Value (Utility)

- Is the product a luxury item or necessity?
- What need does the product(s) fill for the customer? What factors increase/decrease the customer's need for the product?
- Does the product save the customer money?
- Does the product improve efficiency for the customer?
- What alternatives does the customer have?

## Project Profitability

- What is the profitability (gross margins) of each major project type?

# Retail

- Is the company managing its supply chain with a Web-based system?

# Service Features

- What are the top five features of this service?
- What could be considered proprietary features?
- Have there been any reviews/comparisons of the service?
- How sensitive is the customer to service quality?

# Service Life Cycle

- At what stage in the service life cycle is each of the company's core services?

# Service Profitability

- What is the sales volume for each service?
- What is the profitability (gross margin) of each service?
- Is there a relationship between a service's sales/profitability ranking and incentives for salespeople?

# Service Value/Utility

- Is the service a luxury item or necessity?
- What need does the service fill for the customer? What factors increase/decrease the customer's need for the service?
- Does the service save the customer money?
- Does the service improve efficiency for the customer?

- What alternatives does the customer have?

## Subscription Services

- Does the company have in place the necessary mediation software that can collect both Internet protocol (IP) and legacy voice information from a combination of network elements?
  [(a) routers; (b) switches; (c) databases; (d) directory services]

- Is the company using the data collected from mediation to support Billing, Abuse Management, Decision Support, Traffic Engineering, CRM, Service Assurance, and Provisioning?

- Is the company using the data collected from mediation to deliver flexible billing packages based on usage?
  [(a) billing by total upstream or downstream, average or peak throughput levels (Mbps); (b) destination-sensitive billing; (c) billing by total bandwidth used per application (megabytes consumed for Web, streaming, e-mail, etc.); (d) total quantity used per application (number of e-mail sent, Web sites visited, files downloaded, etc.); (e) variable billing for premium and/or free Web sites by quantity of hits or volume used]

# Risk Management

COLI (Corporate-Owned Life Insurance)
Crisis Management
Embezzlement
Emergency Disaster Plans
Fingerprint Authentication
General Liability & Property Insurance
Insurance Coverage
Key Man Life Insurance
Professional Liability Insurance
Property Loss Prevention
Risks
Safety
Self Insurance
Terrorism
Theft
Threat Management
Volatility
Weather Derivatives

## COLI (Corporate-Owned Life Insurance)

- What is the company's policy on COLI? Are there any problems which need to be addressed?

## Crisis Management

- Has the company rehearsed its responses to various crises?

- Does the company carry business interruption insurance?

## Embezzlement

- Has the company ever been a victim of embezzlement?
- What proactive measures are taken within the company to prevent embezzlement?

## Emergency Disaster Plans

- Does the company have a written plan kept off-site to guide the restart of the business in the event of major fire, flood, or other catastrophe of nature?
- Are the appropriate people trained in the implementation of the plan?

## Fingerprint Authentication

- Has the company considered the cost-effectiveness of fingerprint authentication for access to certain company facilities and select rooms?

## General Liability & Property Insurance

- Does the company annually take bids to control costs?
- Can a rigorous safety program reduce premium costs?
- Is the policy "claims made" as "as occurred"?

## Insurance Coverage

- In the event of due diligence on the company, are the details of all insurance coverages reasonably accessible in one location?

[(a) type: health, life, disability, auto, libel, etc.; (b) carrier; (c) limits; (d) premium; (e) pending claims]

- How frequently does the company review coverages?

- Has management evaluated the solvency of its insurance carriers?

- Has the company evaluated the cost-effectiveness of a self-insurance plan?

- Is the company adequately insured for full replacement costs of assets in the case of disaster?

- Is the company adequately insured for all contingent liabilities?

- Are increased premiums anticipated as a result of unfavorable trends or the need for increased coverage?

## Key Man Life Insurance

- Does the company have life insurance on its key officers? Disability insurance?

## Professional Liability Insurance

- Is it possible to transition to a self-insured fund, and if so, what threshold dollar amount is required to proceed?

## Property Loss Prevention

- Does the company have a proactive strategy for property loss prevention?

## Risks

- What are the key areas where the company has, or could have in the future, the greatest risk exposure?
  [(a) strategic blunders; (b) bad acquisitions; (c) environmental

disasters; (d) product and service failures; (e) salesman churning customers' accounts; (f) misuse of derivatives; (g) "cooking the books"; (h) rogue traders; (i) corporate espionage; (j) wrongful discrimination and sexual harassment actions]

- How volatile is the fluctuation in operating results from quarter to quarter?

- How much backlog does the company generally carry?

- Does the company derive a substantial portion of its revenue from a few key customers? What assurances does the company have that sales will continue to these customers? Would a substantial reduction in revenue from these customers adversely affect the company?

- What percentage of sales is to one industry? Would an economic downturn in this industry have an adverse impact on the company?

- Do any of the company's competitors have substantially greater financial, marketing, and technical resources than the company?

- Could competitive pressures or price wars cause the company's products to lose market acceptance?

- How much time delay and cost risk is inherent in the product development process because of technology complexity?

- In spite of testing and QA procedures, is it possible for existing and future products to experience defects or operating deficiencies? What is the risk that the company's product liability exposure could adversely impact cash resources?

- What is the risk to the company's competitive position if it loses its proprietary protection?

- How much dependence on key personnel does the company have?

- Is the company dependent on a few key suppliers?

## Safety

- Is the company a candidate for accreditation under the SA8000 standards (Social Accountability)?
  [(a) child labor; (b) forced labor; (c) health; (d) safety]

## Self Insurance

- Should the company explore the potential cost savings of self insurance?

- How would managed care plans affect the company's self insurance plan?

## Terrorism

- Have we evaluated our exposure to random terrorist activities?

- Are we developing business continuity response plans in that event?

- Can the company feasibly scale down and apply a governmental homeland security model to a multinational corporate model?

## Theft

- What system is in place for reducing the possibility of internal theft?

## Threat Management

- Is the company employing adequate threat management solutions that detect, analyze, and respond to malicious computer attacks, enabling secure and uninterrupted business operations?

# Volatility

- Has the volatility in international markets significantly impacted the company?

# Weather Derivatives

- Could the use of weather derivatives be a cost-effective strategy for mitigating the company's risk exposure due to weather volatility?

# Sales & Customer Service

Backlog
Catalog(s)
Customer Service
Customer Service Ratios
Customer Surveys
80/20 Principle
Manufacturer's Representatives
Questions for Customers
Sales Information
Sales Management
Sales Personnel
Sales Ratios
Sales Territories (Offices)
Sales Training
Time and Expense Tracking
Trade Shows
Travel

## Backlog

- How is backlog defined and computed in the company?

- How does the current backlog compare with the trend for the past two years? As a percentage of net revenue?

- What is the backlog by product line? The trend?

# Catalogs

- What is the company's catalog management strategy? Is it optimizing the balance between hardcopy and online formats?

# Customer Service

- Does the company's workforce management system integrate all key functions to optimize employee performance, and therefore the customer experience?
- What are the top service complaints?
- What have been the most costly complaints?
- What is the trend in customer complaints?
- How does customer service interact with sales?
- Does the company use any third-party providers?
- Is this a profitable operation for the company?
- Is there an excess capacity that can be sold to other companies?
- Does the company have a system in place for automatic response and follow-through to e-mail requests for information and/or customer service?

# Customer Service Ratios

- Customer Satisfaction=[$ total returns/$ sales before returns] %

# Customer Surveys

- Do the organization's predictive intelligence methods and systems provide the capability to test market simulations, anticipate market shifts, and estimate market opportunities?

- How often does the company survey its customers? What methods are used?

# 80/20 Principle

- Can it be said that 20% of our products, or customers, or employees, are really responsible for about 80% of our profits? If this is true, how do we best use this knowledge?
- Which products will yield the highest increase in revenues (profits) for a given investment in product enhancement and/or marketing?
- Which products should we harvest and/or discontinue?

# Manufacturer's Representatives

- Has the standard agreement proven to be effective?
- How does the company evaluate the cost-effectiveness of manufacturer's reps vs. a direct sales force?
- Do any of the company's reps sell competing products?
- What do reps say about the company and its product(s)?
  [(a) product quality; (b) price; (c) ease of sale; (d) customer feedback; (e) suggestions for improvement; (f) treatment and support by the company; (g) payment of commissions; (h) management]

# Questions for Customers

- Do you like the product?
- Has the company lived up to its claim of quality?
- Have you ever been shipped defective goods?
- Has the customer service met your expectations?

- Was the price fair?
- How important is brand identity to you?
- How would you compare the company's product(s) vs. competitors?
- Will you buy from the company again? How much will you spend?
- What changes would you suggest in the product(s)?
- What is your impression of the company's employees?

## Sales Information

- What are the sales breakdowns by various categories?
  [(a) territory; (b) product; (c) customer; (d) industry; (e) application; (f) domestic vs. international]
- What is the size of a typical order? The trend?

## Sales Management

- Is there a sales strategic plan and objectives?
- What is the general sales process?
- What is the general sales compensation plan? Is this compensation plan competitive with the industry?
- What reports are the most effective at managing the sales force?
- How is sales productivity measured?
- How is sales training conducted? Is the cost of training reasonable?

## Sales Personnel

- How important is in-person selling to sell the customer?

- What level of competence is required in salespeople?

- Who are the top salespeople for the company? How long have these individuals been with the company? What are the ages of the top performers?

- What is the average salary plus commissions of the top performers?

- What is the average sales volume of the top performers?

- Have the top performers met their quotas?

- Are competent sales personnel available?

# Sales Ratios

- How do the company's ratios compare with industry norms?

- What is the three-year trend in these ratios?

- Sales Productivity

- [# leads closed / # leads qualified] %

- [$ repeat sales / $ total sales] %

- [$ total sales / # sales people] $

- [# sales / # sales people] %

- Cost Per Sale = [$ selling expenses / $ total sales] %
  [(a) payroll plus benefits; (b) travel; (c) entertainment; (d) commissions]

- Direct Selling Costs = [$ total sales salaries / $ gross sales] %

- Transaction Size = [$ gross sales / # of sales] $

## Sales Territories (Offices)

- How are sales distributed among the following?
  [(a) end user; (b) domestic reps; (c) domestic distributors; (d) intl. distributors; (e) OEM's; (f) other]

- Are all the sales offices producing enough to justify maintaining?

- Is the geographical area served reasonable for each office?

## Sales Training

- Does the company have an effective and ongoing sales training program in place?

## Time and Expense Tracking

- Is the company making use of the advantages of a Web-based time and expense tracking system?

- Does the time tracking system integrate with most of the major accounting systems?

## Trade Shows

- How does the company evaluate the marketing effectiveness of its top three trade shows where the company exhibits?

## Travel

- How does the company optimize its travel expenses?

- How are new technologies being applied such as the web and teleconferencing to reduce the costs of travel?

# *About the Author*

**Scott S. Pickard** is a writer living in Champaign, IL. Scott produces and maintains several dynamic e-books online at **www.scottpickard.com**. He provides a free e-notification service when new content is posted.

## Fiction

*Copper Nation*—On a lonely desert night in the black mountains of New Mexico, a renegade scientist discovers a long-lost secret of the cliff-dwellers that transforms his body and his life forever. But his secret is worth billions to drug lords that would kill and destroy anybody and anything that gets in their path until they bring "the dust" under their control. He forms a blood-pact with two friends to capitalize on this dark fortune, but it is a triad they would live to regret. > **www.coppernation.com**

*Boy Flyer*—Forty years ago on a warm Texas night, two brothers dared each other to an incredible leaping stunt that was their secret for years into manhood. Then strange things began happening to one brother that haunted his dreams and eventually destroyed his career, his marriage, his entire life. And then one day, he mysteriously disappears. > **www.boyflyer.com**

*Olympic Fusion*—In 1980 at the Winter Olympic Games in Lake Placid, Colonel Nikolai Davidov came very close to bringing the Olympic community, and even the world, to its knees. He failed, but he did not give up, and now his plan is on schedule to try once again at the Summer Games in Athens, 2004, to reveal to the world the terrible power of the Black Dove. > **www.olympicfusion.com**

*Sun Runners*—"She could not help but fantasize an extrapolated future of immense scope and wealth that could be generated from the solar chimney should it be successful, and she imagined herself at the center of this wealth and power like some type of energy czar. But the warm wash of the sun on her skin magnified by the helicopter windshield kept her day dream in check, reminding her that it all originated with the sun before her, and would end with the sun after her, and in between she was simply the lucky executor of a solar will written long, long ago." > **www.sunrunners.com**

# Nonfiction

*Due Diligence List*—The Due Diligence List is a reformatted version of *Leaders Ask Good Questions*, with over 2,000 due diligence questions organized under fourteen major functional headings. > **www.duediligencelist.com**

*Forecasting Spreadsheet*—A complete how-to manual for building and maintaining an Excel-based forecasting spreadsheet for the business which can generate: short-term and long-term projections; cash flow; proformas; easy what-if capabilities; executive dashboard of key indicators. > **www.forecastingspreadsheet.com**

*Humor Free*—A regular humor/satire column that makes clean fun of everything and everybody. > **www.humor-free.com**

*Ideas & Queries*—A collection of new product, method, and content ideas to stimulate new idea brainstorming. > **www.ideasandqueries.com**

*Leaders Ask Good Questions*—A thinking tool that has over 2,000 good corporate governance and due diligence questions to keep CEOs on their toes. > **www.askgoodquestions.com**

*Notebook for a Lifetime Learner*—A master outline to help guide the lifetime reader and learner to put knowledge in context. >
**www.notebookforlife.com**

0-595-26130-2